BUY BU

The Fast-Track Strategy to Make Extra Money and Start a Business in Your Spare Time

***

Nick Loper

Copyright and Disclaimer

This book is intended for informational purposes only.

This book includes information, products, and services by third parties. These Third-Party Materials consist of products and opinions expressed by their owners. As such, the author does not assume responsibility or liability for any Third-Party material or opinions.

The publication of such Third-Party Materials does not constitute the author's guarantee of any information, instruction, opinion, products, or services contained within the Third-Party Material. The use of recommended Third-Party Material does not guarantee any success and/or earnings related to you or your business. Publication of such Third-Party Material is simply a recommendation and an expression of the author's own opinion of that material.

Links to Third-Party Resources may be affiliate links, meaning the author may receive compensation if a service is ultimately purchased from such a link.

No part of this publication shall be reproduced, transmitted, or sold in whole or in part in any form without the prior written consent of the author. All trademarks and registered trademarks appearing in this book are the property of their respective owners.

Users of this guide are advised to do their own due diligence when it comes to making business decisions and all information, products, and services that have been provided should be independently verified by your own qualified professionals. By reading this guide, you agree that the author is not responsible for the success or failure of your business or investment decisions relating to any information presented in this book.

Reader Bonus

As a small token of gratitude for you reading this book, I've compiled a few bonuses for you. These are meant to complement the content of the book, help you save money, and take a deeper dive into the business models you're most interested in.

- $1150 in free "sharing economy" discounts and credits.
- The Freelancing and Consulting Bonus: How to get your first clients and position yourself for big paydays.
- The Online Teaching Bonus: How to get paid to share your expertise with others.
- The Ecommerce Bonus: How to start a profitable business selling products online.

To download your free bonuses, you head over to **BuyButtonsBook.com/bonus.**

Introduction

"It was the best of times, it was the worst of times, it was the age of wisdom, it was the age of foolishness, it was the epoch of belief, it was the epoch of incredulity, it was the season of Light, it was the season of Darkness, it was the spring of hope, it was the winter of despair ..."

–Charles Dickens

(*A Tale of Two Cities*, 1859)

Dickens wrote those words more than 150 years ago, yet don't they sound oddly accurate today?

Depending on who you talk to, what news you read, or what channels you watch, this is either the greatest time in history to be alive, or the world is about to end and we're all doomed.

Check out what my new phone can do!

Fifty people liked my last Instagram pic!

I can't wait to binge on the new House of Cards!

But meanwhile:

We're up to our eyeballs in debt!

Governments are on the brink of collapse!

All our jobs are being automated and outsourced!

The Problem

I get where the negativity is coming from, especially from an economic perspective. Real inflation-adjusted wages haven't risen in 30 years, yet our biggest budget items, like housing, transportation, and education, all cost 30-150% more. Job security sounds like an oxymoron.

Half of American households have less than $5,000 saved for retirement. Even scarier, 47% don't have enough cash on hand to cover an unexpected $400 bill, like a car repair. On average, we carry thousands of dollars in high-interest credit card debt.

How do you stack up?

It's easy to feel powerless, like the system is rigged against you. But rigged or not, no one else is going to change it for you. You *can* beat the system, but you're going to have to change your approach.

And that's where the "best of times" part comes in. Despite all the gloom-and-doom and fear-mongering in the news, we are in the middle of an entrepreneurial renaissance. We're nearing an all-time high in new business activity, and economists expect fully half the workforce to be freelancers or self-employed by 2020.

Once viewed as the risky and reckless alternative to a "stable" career at a respected company, entrepreneurship is now seen as a "good career choice" by two-thirds of adults worldwide. One in five of those adults plans to start a new business in the next three years.

Whether this shift is voluntary or reactive, or positive or negative is irrelevant; it's happening. The wheels are already in motion. My friend put it this way: "We're all already entrepreneurs. If you have a day job, your boss is simply your largest client."

The fact is we have more control—and have to *take* more control—over our financial well-being than at any other point in history.

A wise man once said there are only two ways to get rich: make more or desire less. Now this isn't a book about saving money, frugal living, or extreme couponing. I just want you to be aware that there are two sides of the equation.

But here's the thing: since there's only so much you can do to reduce your spending, I like to focus on the income side.

Most people look at their incomes as fixed. There's even a phrase for it: "I'm on a fixed income."

Baloney!

This book is about how to "unfix" your income. The truth is there is more opportunity today to earn income in your spare time than ever before. Your income is never fixed; in fact, it's limitless. The more people you help, the more you can earn. And you don't need a killer new business idea or millions of dollars in startup capital to do it.

The Solution

This book will share specifics on how to *increase* your earning power–on your own time, on your own terms, and without getting another job. We'll look at real-life examples of people just like you making it happen.

And spoiler alert: there are no get-rich-quick schemes inside. Instead, you'll learn proven strategies for tapping into the growing peer-to-peer economy to supplement your income, diversify your revenue sources, and reduce your reliance on your day job for your livelihood.

Because you're reading this book, I know you're serious about improving your situation, earning more money, and building a happier life.

In surveying thousands of people like you who are trying to earn money outside of a day job, 3 consistent challenges come up again and again:

1. Time – I don't have enough time!
2. Ideas – I don't have the right business idea!
3. Money – I don't have enough money to start a business!

To address these, I'm going to arm you with dozens of income-generating ideas that don't require a ton of time or money to get started.

I'm going to focus on marketplaces that already exist, where you can put your expertise, time, and assets up for sale or rent. There are hundreds of platforms that you can add your "buy buttons" to.

You don't have to build a customer base from scratch, design a website, or even worry about payment processing. Each platform already has an audience of buyers looking for what you have to sell.

These platforms are the "gateway drugs" of entrepreneurship. They're easy to get started on, to get the high from your first sale, and to keep coming back for more.

This isn't your traditional entrepreneurship book, and these may not be the types of businesses you typically think of. But they're working, and they're profitable.

You'll meet Jeff Yenisch, an engineer in Tampa, Florida, who is earning $1,500 profit per month renting out his vehicles on the peer-to-peer car rental site Turo.com.

You'll meet Alexandra Kenin, a marketing manager and editor, who hosts $49 urban hikes in San Francisco in her spare time. Alexandra hosted more than 1,000 hikers last year, many of whom connected with her through travel and tour sites like TripAdvisor.com and Viator.com.

You'll meet Carrie Olsen, who started bidding on voice-over jobs on Voices.com. Today she's a full-time voice-over actress, often earning thousands of dollars per job and working with well-known brands like REI and Disneyworld.

You'll meet Kat Parrella, a former IT worker in New York, who now makes a full-time living as a graphic artist, thanks in part to her success on Zazzle.com.

You'll meet Ryan Finlay, who paid off $20,000 of debt and now supports a family of 7 by buying and selling items on Craigslist.

We'll explore some of the most popular marketplaces–plus some lesser-known options–and dive into the best practices for getting started and making your first sales.

By the end of this book, you'll have the information, inspiration, and direction you need to take action and begin earning extra cash on your own schedule. How much you earn and how much time you invest are completely up to you. But know this: the buyers are out there, and I'll show you how to get in front of them.

Why Me?

As an entrepreneur, I've been tapping into the power of marketplaces for over a decade.

One of my first experiences with the "buy buttons" phenomenon was with a house-painting business I ran in college. Over the course of two summers, my crew and I painted 50-60 houses and did $150,000 worth of business.

The first year, my main marketing channel was good old-fashioned cold calling. After class, I'd drive out to my territory, knock on doors, and schedule estimates for the upcoming weekend.

The problem with cold calling is it's super inefficient. Yes, I could get directly in front of the homeowners (my target customer), but they weren't in "buying mode," and only a small percentage were in the market for a new paint job.

The next year, a little older and wiser, I was determined to cut back on the cold-calling drudgery. How could I more efficiently get in front of homeowners interested in home improvement? I happened to find out about an event called the Seattle Home Show and registered a display booth.

At the convention, hundreds of vendors were competing for attention, but there were also thousands and thousands of homeowners walking the aisles, looking to spend money on their houses.

(A college kid perched on a ladder, waving a sign, was a great attention-getting tactic.)

In just 4 days, my partners and I collected dozens of leads and ended up booking more than $70,000 worth of work. It was an eye-opening experience about the power of going where your target customers already are and putting up your "buy button."

Since then, I've used the same marketplace strategy over and over again. When I sold shoes online, I took out targeted ads on Google for shoe-related search terms. When I began selling digital products and freelancing services, I set up shop on Fiverr.com. When I created an online course, I put it up for sale on Udemy.com.

When I launched my podcast, I made sure to syndicate it to iTunes. Even when I'm trying to sell stuff in our garage, I turn to marketplaces like eBay or Craigslist.

In fact, with this very book I'm tapping into Amazon's massive audience of buyers to sell more copies.

Marketplaces are all around us; you probably use a ton of them every month without even thinking about it. In the pages that follow, I'll open your eyes to new income opportunities right under your nose and hopefully spark some creative ideas you never thought of before.

Real People, Real Results

Through *The Side Hustle Show* podcast, I've interviewed more than 150 awesome entrepreneurs, and the show has been downloaded more than 1.5 million times. A common theme of the show is to tap into pre-existing marketplaces to earn extra money on the side and to jumpstart a larger business.

What's most exciting to me, though, is that people are listening and taking action.

Kevin is an attorney-turned-entrepreneur. In just the first two months of selling his book on Amazon, he earned $2,000 and added 500 new email subscribers to his list.

Dan works a "dead-end job" (his words) as an office assistant, but earned $3,000 in his first three months reselling products on eBay.

Aja is an IT consultant in Chicago and has been building her side income teaching courses on Udemy.com. She earns $300 a month from her video courses.

Jesse is a professional stage hypnotist who has earned thousands of dollars winning copywriting jobs in his spare time on Upwork.com.

Gina runs an ecommerce store, but made over $25,000 in nine months renting her Ireland flat on Airbnb.

Assad is a finance director by day, who made over $100,000 on the side in less than 12 months reselling products on Amazon.

The common thread is they all set up their businesses on pre-existing platforms that made it easy for buyers to find them and spend money with them. This book will show you exactly how they—and dozens of others—set up their "buy buttons" to generate substantial side income.

My Guarantee

In the coming pages, I guarantee you'll find at least one "buy button" platform that you can use to generate your own job-free income stream. If you don't, just send me a note (my contact info is at the end of the book), and I'll buy the book back from you, no questions asked.

Now, where else are you going to find a deal like that?

Ready? Let's get started!

Table of Contents

The Power of Marketplaces

"Because that's where the money is."

—Willie Sutton (on why he robbed banks)

A marketplace is simply a place for buyers and sellers to connect. We've been building marketplaces for thousands of years, from the Agora of ancient Greece to Amazon today.

When my wife and I visited Istanbul last year, we walked through the Grand Bazaar. In continuous operation for more 500 years and home to over 4,000 vendors, the Grand Bazaar claims to be the world's first shopping mall.

In your town, you probably have similar marketplaces on a smaller scale: farmer's markets, swap meets, flea markets, street fairs, city-wide garage sales, etc. Each of these is an example of buyers connecting with sellers.

In the past 20 years—and even in the past 5 years—we've witnessed an explosion of "niche" marketplaces that specialize in very specific transactions.

Need to rent a boat? BoatBound.co has you covered.

Need a logo designed for your business? Check out DesignCrowd.com.

Want to learn Portuguese for your trip to Brazil next summer? Verbling.com can help.

While this book focuses primarily on online marketplaces and mobile apps, I've included "local" marketplaces for your consideration as well. Many of these facilitate the exchange of goods and services among neighbors, which is a great way to connect with buyers right in your hometown.

(And if you don't live in or near a big city, that's where the "virtual," location-independent options come in.)

In this book you'll learn about marketplaces grouped into 3 main categories:

1. The Sharing Economy
2. Marketplaces for Selling Skills
3. Marketplaces for Selling Physical Products

The first group is the sharing economy. These platforms and apps aim to "cut out the middleman" in all sorts of transactions. In this section, you'll discover nearly 200 sharing economy marketplaces, and you'll meet entrepreneurs and side hustlers who are taking advantage of them.

The next section covers marketplaces to sell your skills. Whether you have a broad range of skills or are highly specialized, odds are there's a platform dedicated to your industry or expertise. And if you don't think you have any skills worth selling, this section will give you some ideas and confidence as well.

The third category is marketplaces where you can sell physical products. Despite an increasingly digital world, we still shop for physical goods all the time. This section reviews some of the most exciting and active opportunities for tapping into this massive audience of buyers.

Two-sided markets are really hard to build. After all, there's no reason for sellers to set up shop if there aren't any buyers, and no reason for buyers to stop by if there aren't any sellers. The marketplaces listed in this book face the same challenges, but have generally gotten past that initial stage of attracting a critical mass of both parties.

When there are more buyers than there are sellers to meet the demand, that's a great time to be a seller, and you can command higher prices. And on the flipside, if a marketplace is flooded with sellers, that tends to drive prices down in competitive bidding wars.

In each marketplace featured, we'll look at ways to make your Buy Buttons stand out and get attention.

Why Marketplaces are so Powerful for Sellers

Imagine starting an ice cream shop on a deserted highway. You've got the best ice cream in the world, a great selection of flavors, and a beautiful new parlor. You've poured your blood, sweat, and tears into getting this business off the ground, perfecting the recipes, buying all the fancy equipment, and selecting the right seats and signage.

But no one knows about your shop, and worse, no one ever drives by to discover it.

Within a week, your hopes are dashed, and you think you're just not cut out to be an entrepreneur.

It sounds silly, but I see too many people make these same mistakes when they start their businesses. They put all this time, effort, energy, and money into building a website to be "open for business." They're buying into the "build it and they will come" theory, but this isn't *Field of Dreams*.

Instead of setting up shop in that proverbial corn field in Iowa, why not put your Buy Button where customers are *already* shopping? Instead of that ice cream shop in the middle of nowhere, put yours at a prime downtown location on a hot summer day.

Today's marketplaces give you the power to do just that. On day one, your offerings are visible to hundreds, thousands, or even millions of potential buyers. Never before was this kind of accelerated launch available—and at zero or very little startup cost.

Mini Search Engines

Think of these platforms as their own mini search engines. You don't have to compete with the entirety of the Internet for attention.

Getting on the first page of Google's results is hard, but getting on the first page of results on a niche marketplace is much more attainable. And each marketplace is a potential new avenue of discovery and revenue for you and your business.

Look at the example of Airbnb. Twenty years ago, if you wanted to rent out a spare room in your house or turn your apartment into a vacation rental, how would you get in front of potential customers? A sign in the yard? A classified ad in the paper?

By building an active marketplace, Airbnb has effectively unlocked an untapped revenue stream for property owners.

Mindset shift: Every transaction has a buyer and a seller. Put yourself on the other side of the equation. What can you sell?

This shift from consumer to creator is an exciting one. It's an empowering moment when you earn your first job-free dollars. It's a meaningful act of financial independence.

Many of these marketplaces fall under the umbrella of the sharing economy, and that's where we'll start our journey.

The Sharing Economy

"All our relationships are person-to-person. They involve people seeing, hearing, touching, and speaking to each other; they involve sharing goods; and they involve moral values like generosity and compassion."

—Brendan Myers

What is the Sharing Economy?

Some call it the sharing economy, some call it the on-demand economy, and some call it collaborative consumption. No matter what you call it, it's massively impacting how we do business while also disrupting established industries at a breakneck speed.

I'm talking about the renaissance of people doing business with people—a movement facilitated by an ever-growing array of marketplaces and apps.

If we think back in time 200 years, almost all commerce was peer-to-peer, right? We traded in small town squares and knew our neighbors. Then, big corporations came in and took over the world. In a sense, the "sharing economy"—with the help of websites and apps—is helping us return to our roots with a new wave of person-to-person connections, interactions, and transactions.

The premise is that we have *underutilized assets* in our lives (our house, car, stuff, expertise, time, money, etc.), and we can sell or rent those to our neighbors in win-win transactions.

Economic Impact

These app-powered, peer-to-peer transactions will unlock an estimated *$300 billion* in economic activity by 2025. That's up from $15 billion in 2013, according to PricewaterhouseCoopers. So don't make the mistake of thinking you've missed the boat. We're still in the early days of this economic shift.

Want your piece of the pie?

This section is all about how you can get in on the action.

One in five American adults has already participated as a seller in the sharing economy, while nearly half have used the services as a buyer.

Sharing economy participants skew younger and more educated than the general population, but there are opportunities for all ages, regardless of education.

Flexibility and Opportunity

Sharing economy workers earn a median of $18 an hour, according to a 2014 Stanford 1099 survey, almost a dollar more than the $17.09 median for all occupations, as reported by the Bureau of Labor Statistics in May 2014. This means that if you put in just an hour a day and earn that median rate, you would earn an extra $500 a month or $6,000 a year.

In this section, we'll look at several examples from the sharing economy, some of which earn much more than that $18 an hour rate. Unsurprisingly, the bigger, rarer, or more valuable the asset you're sharing, the more you stand to earn.

According to a *Time* magazine survey, half of sharing economy sellers reported being better off financially and were significantly more optimistic about their future prospects than were their non-sharing counterparts.

The "average" sharing economy seller–if there is such a thing–puts in just 10 hours a month. In fact, more than 90% of sellers are part-timers, making it a fantastic and proven way to earn money while still keeping your full-time job.

And perhaps that is the biggest selling point of all: the power to earn money on your own terms and on your own time without going "all in" and quitting your job to start a business.

Among sharing economy workers, 43% say they prefer the independence of on-demand work–even at the expense of job security and benefits. (In fairness, a nearly equal percentage reported being willing to give up that independence for a more stable job.)

Still, many participants are attracted to the flexibility and freedom of setting their own hours. A recent Uber driver of mine in Chicago explained it best: "When I want to make money, I turn on the app."

Reputation Metrics

The sharing economy is built on a foundation of trust. In practice this usually entails a two-sided user rating system in which buyers rate sellers and sellers rate buyers.

This gives sellers incentive to provide a great service, be polite, and make an honest representation of what they're offering. If they fail in any one of those areas, customers will rate them poorly. They'll either have to step up their game, or they'll have a hard time landing clients on the platform.

On Uber for example, drivers must maintain a 4.6-star rating (out of 5), or they risk getting kicked off the app.

Similarly, buyers get rated too. If I'm a total jerk or if I trash my Airbnb rental, my host will leave me a bad rating, and it will be harder for me to complete my next booking. (The host is also protected by a $1 million liability insurance policy.)

Because of this, both parties actually have a great reason to be kind to each other. Maybe this will ultimately lead to a more civil and friendly society!

To be sure, there are plenty of downsides and risks to the sharing economy as well. But before we dive into those, I want to share some of the potential platforms you can use to begin earning job-free income.

What can you share? Let's find out!

Sharing Economy Platforms

This section features nearly 200 different sharing economy platforms in order to show you just how broad this space is. Some of these will be familiar household names like Uber and Airbnb, but many will likely be new to you.

In fact, the sharing economy goes much deeper than just renting out extra space or driving people around your city. This section will help get your creative juices flowing by uncovering dozens of marketplaces you may be able to add your Buy Buttons to.

One thing to keep in mind is that many of these companies are startups and may only be available in select cities and countries at the moment. I focused on English-language platforms, but often you can find similar options in your area by searching around or by reaching out to the platform you like and offering to help it expand to your area.

Following the theme of underutilized assets, this section is organized in alphabetical order by the asset you're sharing. Some of these platforms are admittedly a little off the wall, but that's part of the fun!

Share Your Boat

With **Boatbound.co** you can rent your boat to your landlocked peers. A quick search of boats nearby yielded plenty of results with rates ranging from $230 to $950 per day! How often do you *really* get out on the water?

Other Platforms to Consider

GetMyBoat – GetMyBoat.com is another peer-to-peer boat rental platform with listings all around the world.

Sailsquare – Travelers can participate in sailing experiences directly offered by private sailboat owners. Skippers are charging $500 and up per passenger per week, and Sailsquare.com says it has 30,000 users on the platform.

Tubbber | Boaterfly | Antlos – These platforms provide peer-to-peer boat rentals, primarily in Europe.

Share Your Car

Ridesharing Services

Uber is the proverbial 800-pound gorilla of the sharing economy. The pioneering ridesharing platform essentially enables you to start your own taxi service and earn money on your own schedule driving your neighbors around.

Drivers report earning anywhere from $12-25 an hour.

New to Uber? Get $20 off your first ride at sidehustlenation.com/uber.

Lyft – If your car qualifies for Uber, you might as well join Lyft, too. This ridesharing service is branded more as "your friend with a car" and is perhaps a little more personable than the Uber behemoth. Because of that, I actually prefer Lyft as a rider.

New to Lyft? Get $50 in free ride credits at sidehustlenation.com/lyft.

BlaBlaCar – This European ridesharing service gives you the chance to fill your empty seats on that upcoming road trip and offset some of your travel costs.

Wingz – Wingz.me drivers only do airport pick-ups and drop-offs, with flat fares and no surge pricing. You can also develop relationships with customers who can then request rides directly from you. According to the site, top drivers are bringing in $2,000 a week.

Scoop – The TakeScoop.com carpooling app connects you with other commuters heading in your direction and allows you to share the costs. It's an interesting twist on the ridesharing concept since it focuses on a trip you're making anyway—driving to work. Plus, your income is tax free because it's categorized as a reimbursement rather than a fare.

Vugo – While not specifically a ridesharing app, the free Vugo app at GoVugo.com entertains your rideshare passengers with "relevant media and contextual ads" and gives drivers an easy way to electronically accept tips via PayPal. The promise is incremental revenue from rides you're already driving.

Peer-to-Peer Car Rental Services

The Side Hustle Show listener Jeff Yenisch sent me a note about the success he's having with the peer-to-peer car rental service Turo. If driving people around Uber-style isn't your jam, you might consider this as an alternative. Your car probably sits idle at least some of the time, and Turo wants to help make that idle time work for you.

Jeff, an engineer in Tampa, reports earning $1,500 profit a month on Turo in just 2-4 hours a week. "My location has some built-in advantages with the local tourism industry," he explained. "Most of my customers fly in from out of state, and we live somewhat close to two airports."

He told me he stumbled across the service last year when trying to find a 3-month rental car for an intern at work. Since the intern was under 25 and from France, the traditional rental car companies wanted to charge him over $1,500 a month for an economy car. "I came across Turo while researching options for him," Jeff said, "and decided to give it a try myself."

Sensing there was an opportunity, Jeff purchased an older Ford Escape from a repo man and rented it out for several months after the intern returned to France. "It was a cash cow," he said.

Jeff listed his wife's Mazda CX-9, a 7-passenger SUV, on the site to see if there would be any interest. It's rented out almost full time now.

"SUVs have a strong demand with many families visiting here," he said, "And it's easy to undercut the SUV prices of the traditional rental car companies and still make a nice revenue figure, rather than settling for smaller margins with an economy car."

This spring, Jeff decided to scale up this side hustle by adding more inventory. "I leased two brand new Chevy Equinoxes," he explained. "I was a little nervous adding $500 in lease payments for these two cars to my bottom line, but the demand has been very good." Jeff said these new additions to his "fleet" bring in an extra $1500 in monthly revenue.

He mentioned that another advantage working in his favor is that he travels for his day job quite a bit. "We rarely need two cars at any given time," Jeff explained. "My wife is a stay-at-home mom and helps with handling some of the car pickups when I'm gone."

I was curious about the time investment required to meet customers, hand over the keys, and perform check-in inspections. Jeff said, "Between the three cars, there are usually 2-3 meet-ups per week to deliver or pick up cars at the airport. Considering the revenue, it's a very low time commitment." He added that most rentals are at least a week, and he's had a few that were over a month.

"I think a side hustle with Turo would work for a lot of people," Jeff said. "The platform is only going to grow as more travelers learn about it."

Turo carries a $1 million liability insurance policy on each vehicle and covers damage or theft up to the actual cash value of your car.

Naturally, newer cars in popular travel destinations earn the most, and Turo even has a cool little calculator on its site to estimate how much you might earn.

Other Platforms to Consider

GetAround – GetAround.com is a similar concept to Turo, and has car owners earning up to $10,000 a year and rental periods as short as one hour. There's no rule that says you can't list on both markets, but you'll just have to remember to update the availability calendar if certain dates get booked on one platform and not the other.

Outdoorsy – Rent out your RV on the Outdoorsy.co peer-to-peer marketplace and earn $150-$350 per day. The company handles bookings and payments, and carries $1 million in insurance should anything happen to your rig on the open road.

Want to ride? Get $100 off your first rental at sidehustlenation.com/outdoorsy.

Car Next Door – The leading peer-to-peer car rental service in Australia is currently guaranteeing car owners they'll earn $2,000 in their first 12 months on the platform if they meet certain sign-up criteria.

easyCar Club – Earn up to £3,000 a year with this UK-based, peer-to-peer car hire service.

Vehicle Advertising Services

When you sign up with **Wrapify.com**, your car gets covered with a giant advertisement, and you earn money based on how far you drive. A typical commuter in a popular area could earn $50-100 a week.

Side Hustle Nation reader Janet Saunderson, a project manager in Chicago, reported earning around $400 a month with Wrapify "just for driving where I'd normally be driving!"

Similarly, if you have a 2005 model year car or newer and drive 800+ miles a month, you may qualify to earn $300-650 per campaign with **Carvertise.com**. The company has been around since 2012 and is one of the more established players in this space.

Delivery Services

Tyler Castleman is a part-time lawyer and mother of 6 in Birmingham, Alabama. She delivers groceries with **Shipt.com** in her spare time to supplement her income.

Shipt primarily serves cities in the southern US, though similar services operate regionally throughout the country and in different parts of the world. According to Shipt, shoppers can earn $15-25 an hour picking up and delivering groceries.

"It's enabled me to not only make some extra money for my family, but also to feel like I'm helping people and meeting new people all the time," Tyler explained.

Robert Murray reported earning $3,000 a month as a part-time Shipt shopper in Miami, and said he used the extra money to buy a new car.

In Minneapolis, attorney Kevin Ha earns side hustle income making bicycle deliveries with the Postmates.com app. "I enjoy biking and need the exercise, so if I feel like getting an hour or two of exercise in, I'll just hop on Postmates and make some deliveries," he explained. "I can usually make about $15 an hour, and am on pace to make about $2,500 this year, all for something I enjoy doing in my spare time—with the added health benefit of biking around town."

Other Platforms to Consider

Instacart – Get paid to shop for and deliver other people's groceries.

Shyp – In select cities you can earn money picking up and shipping packages.

Washio – Become a Washio "ninja" and help pick up and deliver laundry and dry cleaning in your neighborhood.

Sprig – Deliver meals for Sprig (no cooking required) and get a free meal yourself each shift, in addition to getting paid.

DoorDash – Make $25 an hour as a food delivery driver for DoorDash.com.

Munchery – Earn $20 an hour plus reimbursement for mileage and cellular data delivering meals in your neighborhood.

Saucey – Get paid to deliver alcohol.

Caviar – Earn up to $25 an hour delivering restaurant meals to homes and businesses.

Amazon Flex – Earn $18-25 an hour making deliveries for Amazon in select markets.

Deliv – Deliv.co is another on-demand delivery app where drivers can earn money running errands and delivering goods locally.

Roadie | DropTrip | CitizenShipper – These platforms match travelers with people who need stuff shipped. Got extra room in your trunk? Offset the cost of your trip by delivering something that's heading in the same direction. Gigs pay anywhere from $10 to $1,000, depending on the size of what's being shipped and how far it's going.

Share Your Care

A friend of ours in New York actually connected with a celebrity client on SitterCity.com, a huge marketplace for child care, with parents posting jobs every 2 minutes. She had the summer off from her teaching job and was looking to earn some extra cash. She ended up with a great nanny position and has built a long-term relationship with the family.

Other Platforms to Consider

Care.com – With more than 19 million members, Care.com is the largest marketplace for child care, senior care, pet care, and house sitting.

UrbanSitter – If you love kids, this could be the perfect side hustle. Set your own babysitting rates, availability, and geographic area you cover. Because UrbanSitter.com charges parents a monthly membership fee to access the directory, you keep 100% of your earnings.

Talkspace – Talkspace.com is the platform where you can chat directly with licensed therapists on demand. On the flip side, if you're a licensed therapist, you can set up your profile and begin earning up to $3,000 a month taking your practice online.

DoulaMatch – Like the name would suggest, DoulaMatch.net is a marketplace for doulas and those seeking them.

MDLive – Board-certified doctors, pediatricians, and therapists can take live patient calls from anywhere on the MDLive.com platform.

Share Your City

On any given weekend in San Francisco, out of earshot from the barking harbor seals at Pier 39 and the clang of the cable cars, a small group of urban hikers are exploring the city from a different vantage point. For three hours, they walk, climb, and even slide their way through historic neighborhoods and scenic outlooks.

They're led by Alexandra Kenin—or one of her carefully selected guides—and have paid $49 apiece for this unique travel experience. Alexandra runs UrbanHikerSF.com on the side from her day job as a content writer and editor.

As a transplant from the East Coast, she often spent her free time exploring her new home on foot, inspired by the book *Stairway Walks in San Francisco*. When she saw companies offering walking tours, bike tours, bus tours, and even Segway tours, she wondered if there would be demand for a hiking tour of the city.

Alexandra mapped out three of her favorite routes and studied the history of different spots along the way. She put up a website, and her first paying customers were actually referred by her dad's wife. With some positive and constructive feedback under her belt, she ran a one-time discount promotion on Zozi.com, a travel site geared toward outdoor experiences.

Two hundred people bought the deal, which netted Alexandra $35 each. That was enough to validate the business, but more importantly, that was enough to begin collecting reviews on other travel platforms, including the granddaddy of them all: TripAdvisor.com.

"On the hikes, I would bring my camera and take pictures of the hikers," Alexandra explained. "Afterwards, I'd send them a thank you note with a link to download all the pictures and ask them to leave a TripAdvisor review."

The reviews helped build up exposure on the TripAdvisor platform, which turned into a virtuous circle of more bookings and more business. "Because I had three hours of personal face time with my customers getting to know them, they were much more likely to leave a review," Alexandra explained. We tend to think that only big companies and fancy hotels can have a presence on TripAdvisor, but there's a peer-to-peer element to it as well.

More than 1,000 people take her urban hikes each year, and she now oversees a team of 4-5 guides who can lead the hikes in her place. (She was in New York when we caught up, earning passive income from this business she's built while hikes were taking place without her.)

In addition to TripAdvisor, she's syndicated her tour offerings to other platforms that cater to travelers, including Vayable.com, Viator.com, and Verlocal.com. "Viator probably accounted for $5k worth of tours last year," Alexandra said, adding that each platform is another way to get in front of a potential customer.

She even participated in a pilot program with Airbnb, where the booking service recommended a curated list of local activities to guests staying in San Francisco.

Urban Hiker SF was an inexpensive business to get off the ground and doesn't have much ongoing overhead. Alexandra took advantage of the pre-existing travel platforms to turn a hobby into a growing side hustle, all while helping thousands of visitors get a unique experience on their trip.

Could you start something similar in your city?

Other Platforms to Consider

GetYourGuide – Become a tour provider in more than 2,300 locations around the world on

GetYourGuide.com and get paid to show off your city to travelers.

ToursByLocals – If you already are a professional tour guide, you can use the ToursByLocals.com platform to connect directly with your customers and earn a better living.

WithLocals – Host food and tour experiences in your city. So far, WithLocals.com has more traction in Europe and Asia.

Govoyagin – Create your own unique local tour experience and get paid when travelers join you. GoVoyagin.com is currently only in Asia.

Rent-a-Guide – With hand-selected tours in more than 100 countries around the world, rent-a-guide.com is another platform where you can create your own travel experiences, set your prices, and accept clients.

Trip4real - Trip4real.com is a trusted community platform that connects locals with travelers from all over the world. With the click of a button, local city-dwellers can offer tours and activities in whatever they are interested in. When I searched options in Prague, I found a beer tour, a museum walk, and a glassblowing exhibition priced from $15-60 per person.

Guidrr – Become a "destination ambassador" on the Guidrr.com app and create your own digital city experience. Creators can earn sponsorship for content and receive paid creation inquiries from brands. The experiences you create are self-guided, so you don't need to be present to cash in.

Getguided.co.uk – This small but growing operation facilitates peer-to-peer tours in select UK cities.

LocalAventura – LocalAventura.com offers authentic, unique, and customizable peer-to-peer travel experiences in Latin America.

MeetnGreetMe – With MeetnGreetMe.com, you can set up shop as a personal travel concierge and earn money "meeting and greeting" visitors at the airport, showing them around town, or making reservations or appointments in the local language.

Blikkee – Earn cash for providing personalized local recommendations to travelers in your neighborhood via text message. Free help is always available, but the most "in the know" locals charge for their recommendations. For instance, Dillon Casey, 23, collects $5 for recommending her favorite spots in Brooklyn, New York.

"I love helping those who visit my neighborhood," she said. "My friends say I give great advice, but this is amazing. I get to meet new people, make money, and save for a trip to Thailand!" Blikkee.com won't make you rich—Dillon has earned a little over $90 so far this year—but is one more way to supplement your income.

Share Your Clothes

Rent your designer clothes (you know, the items that cost $200+ retail) through the Style Lend fashion-sharing platform. The company will store your clothes for free and pay you each time someone rents an item of yours.

Share Your Data?

The startup DataWallet.io promises to let you "reclaim the profits made with your data," including what you choose to share on networks like Facebook, Instagram, and Pinterest.

Choose what you share and what companies you share it with and earn up to $50 each time your data is sold.

Share Your Food

Catherine Nissen earns money hosting dinner parties at her Washington, DC, home. She charges up to $65 a plate on the EatWith.com platform, which aims to "bring chefs and foodies together one meal at a time."

"I can fit 12 people at my table, and another 8 at the counter on high stools," Catherine said. Doing the math, that's up to $1,300 per event when she sells out.

Catherine isn't a professional chef, but said she is using EatWith to change her career. "I'm not completely new to cooking," she explained. "I mentored with a famous Lebanese chef for 8 years, but I do not have culinary school or professional kitchen experience." Still, the former shoe and jewelry designer is having a blast on the platform that lets her express her creativity in a new way.

She experiments with new menus and pairings all the time and loves the "instant gratification" of seeing guests enjoy something she made.

I asked Catherine if she was nervous inviting strangers into her home, but as she pointed out, "Most of the time the guests are more apprehensive," adding that you can approve or decline any reservation requests through the EatWith system. "Nothing ventured, nothing gained," she smiled.

Her most common diners are locals out for a unique first date or for a one-of-a-kind dinner party with friends that they don't have to host. After her first couple of dinners, word began to spread, and repeat customers would bring their friends to try out the latest menu offering.

"Honestly, it all comes down to the pictures," Catherine said, after I asked her what made her listings stand out on the EatWith platform. "We eat with our eyes first, and then our other senses come into play, especially when it's online. I shoot every dish from two angles, and add in some shots of the venue," she explained.

Beyond mouth-watering pictures, Catherine also encourages guests to leave reviews on EatWith, which improves her visibility. One reviewer wrote, "I will be going to her house now for my third time in the past two months, mainly for that coconut rice and to stand in her Pinterest-worthy open kitchen," and added, "What makes this experience so memorable is Catherine's passion for cooking. She's so thoughtful and meticulous about the ingredients she uses, it will inspire you to try something new."

"EatWith allows me to learn to be entrepreneurial—with someone holding my hand on the side if I need it," Catherine explained. To grow her business, she's planning partnerships with local specialty grocery stores and organizing events for local food bloggers and hotel concierges.

How does hosting meals compare with her previous careers? "Cooking is way more fun!" she said. "EatWith gives me the freedom and flexibility to set my own menu, schedule, and dining experience."

Other Platforms to Consider

Feastly – Put your culinary skills up for sale by hosting group meals on the EatFeastly.com platform. One New York chef reported earning $1,000 a month part time on this site.

Bon Appetour – Get paid to cook and host meals for travelers in your home.

VizEat – This meal-sharing marketplace has a strong presence in Europe and works similarly to the others listed here. Craft your own culinary experience, set your price, and host guests when you're available.

MiumMium – This is the Buy Button marketplace for personal chefs and caterers to book dinner parties and other events for local homeowners and hosts. Earn $30-80 per guest depending on your menu.

MealSharing.com – "Make extra money filling your table with new people." You set your menu, prices, and availability, and the Meal Sharing marketplace helps connect you with customers.

CookUnity – Freelance chefs in New York City can join CookUnity.us for access to its kitchen facility and packaging services to reach a new audience of foodies.

Share Your Friendship?

Yes, these sites actually exist.

<u>What's Your Price</u> – Calling all the single ladies! On this unique dating platform, you set your price for a first date and get paid when someone takes you out.

According to the company's blog, women are charging anywhere from $10 to $300 for a night out—and probably getting a meal out of the deal, too.

<u>Rent a Friend</u> – According to RentaFriend.com, you can earn up to $50 an hour on this strictly platonic match-making site. You might get hired to accompany new "friends" to the movies, dinner, the gym, or whatever you include in your free profile.

<u>CuddleUp</u> – CuddleUp is a "cuddling for hire" service. If the options above weren't creepy enough for you, join CuddleUp.com for free, create your profile, and start accepting cuddle requests. In browsing the site, I found rates ranging from free to $99 an hour.

Share Your Goals?

With the free <u>Pact</u> app, you can earn up to $5 a week for staying true to your health goals. This one's on the honor system, though, and your rewards are paid for by the 8% of people who admit to falling off the wagon.

Share Your Good Taste

On Kit.com you can share your favorite items without ever letting them out of your sight.

You simply create a kit (what essentials you bring on every business trip, for example), and make affiliate links to buy the products on Amazon. Earn money whenever someone buys the products you recommend.

Share Your Home

Airbnb is one of the most well-known sharing economy platforms and is disrupting the hotel industry in a big way. You can rent out your entire home, a spare bedroom, an air mattress on your floor, or even a tent in your backyard.

My friend Jasper Ribbers is an Airbnb host in Amsterdam, and he said, "If you have hotels in your city or town, you know there's at least *some* demand." The platform is giving an audience of 60 million travelers a different option to a hotel stay, usually offering more space for less money and a more unique local experience. As for the hosts, Airbnb and similar marketplaces are giving homeowners the chance to unlock extra income from assets they already own and meet people from all over the world.

I'm a fan of Airbnb.com as a user. (I've stayed in Airbnbs in the US, Spain, Portugal, Italy, Turkey, and Japan.) It's definitely a great way to monetize an underutilized asset under your own roof. Your rates are going to be dictated by your local competition, which could be anywhere from $40 to $300 a night.

Janelle Jones, a *Side Hustle Nation* reader from Atlanta, witnessed the power of the Airbnb marketplace right away. Janelle was working as a virtual assistant and part-time tutor, but was looking for ways to earn more income.

"I listed my second bedroom on Airbnb for $50 a night," she explained, adding that her proximity to downtown Atlanta was a big selling point. "I began to get booked up, and I was like, 'Why didn't I do this sooner?'"

Janelle ended up moving in with a friend, so she could rent her condo as an "entire place" listing, charging up to $149 a night. She said the unit now runs at 75-90% occupancy and brings in an average of $3,500 a month.

In New York City, Ben Foley was similarly surprised by the demand on Airbnb. "I listed an air mattress in the living room of our apartment for $80 a night," Ben, a finance associate, said. "We didn't think there'd be people staying with us every night."

After going "gung ho" for a couple months, Ben decided to dial back his hosting and focus only on renting the entire Manhattan apartment while he and his girlfriend were out of town. "Next month we're going to Costa Rica for a couple weeks, and the apartment is already rented for $1600 during that time," he explained. "It covers travel expenses for us, which is pretty cool."

Airbnb provides hosts with a $1 million liability insurance policy for every stay, but the platform also allows you to collect a security deposit and charge a standard cleaning fee. "I charge a $250 security deposit," Janelle explained, "in case guests damage the furniture or the unit itself."

She adds a $60 cleaning fee to each stay, which is passed on directly to the cleaning service that helps turn over the condo between guests.

I asked Ben what he did to protect valuables or other sensitive documents in the apartment while he was away, and he said they have a safe for jewelry and lease a safe deposit box offsite for $80 a year.

In their first 3 months on Airbnb, Ben and his girlfriend earned around $3500. "It's great side income, especially in New York where the cost of living is so high," he said, adding, "It's also a cool way to meet new people; 80% of our guests are international. Now we have friends all over the world."

I was curious how much time hosts spend managing the check-in/check-out process, but in Janelle's case she's automated the whole thing. "Everything is done through electronic keypad. I don't have to meet the guests," she said. While that certainly saves her time, she speculated that the lack of personal interaction is hurting her reviews on the Airbnb platform.

"When I was staying in the other bedroom, I had the chance to build a real relationship and connection with my guests," she explained, adding that that relationship translated into glowing reviews. Jasper, who rents his Amsterdam apartment while traveling the world, found a happy medium where his house cleaner checks guests in and out and provides that personal touch.

In any case, Airbnb has turned into a significant side income for Janelle, Jasper, Ben, and thousands of others around the globe.

Bonus: *Get $30 off your first stay at sidehustlenation.com/airbnb.*

The Next Level: Airbnb Investments

Elizabeth Colegrove and her husband are both under 30, but have amassed a real estate empire of 8 houses and counting. As a Navy family, they've been stationed all around the country and have picked up properties as they've gone.

When I spoke to Elizabeth, they were clearing $1,800 a month in net positive cash flow from this portfolio, which she self-managed remotely. A few months later, she told me they're transitioning a couple of the properties from a 12-month lease strategy to a short-term rental strategy.

"Airbnb has tripled my income," she said, adding that the improved bottom line allowed her to quit her job. "We had to furnish the homes, which cost around $3,000 each, but we made that back within the first two months."

Traditional real estate investors try and abide by "the 1% rule," which states that your monthly rent should be at least 1% of the value of the home and the higher, the better.

For example, if you have a $100,000 home with a monthly rent of $1,000, it fits the bill. The problem is that houses that meet "the 1% rule" can be hard to come by in certain markets. "Our houses have been closer to 0.7% on average," Elizabeth explained. That would be something like a $200,000 house renting for $1400 a month.

But let's say that a $200,000 home could fetch $150 a night as a short-term rental. Even if it's only occupied half the month, that's still an equivalent monthly rent of $2,250. If you were cash-flowing $300 a month from a 12-month lease, all of a sudden that shoots up to $1,150 a month on the 50% vacant Airbnb plan.

Elizabeth found some initial success in the corporate rental market, where companies pay a premium to provide turnkey housing for relocating workers. "One property went from a rent of $1,600 to a furnished corporate rental rate of $4,400," she explained.

However, there are some drawbacks to consider in return for that extra income. Your monthly expenses go up with short-term rentals, you may have to do more hands-on maintenance, and you may have more management time involved in checking guests in and out.

Elizabeth said her costs on that $4,400 rental rose by $700 a month to pay for landscaping, pool maintenance, and the air conditioning bill. Where those extra carrying costs get scary is if you have a vacancy for any length of time.

"With corporate rentals, it's kind of this weird, stressful game of chicken," she explained. "The money is great, but companies can be slow to sign a deal, and you're left wondering if you'd be better off doing one-off vacation rentals." The paydays are bigger, but there's much more stress and anxiety.

Still, if you're evaluating real estate investments, it's worthwhile to evaluate the property from both a long-term and short-term rental standpoint. To learn more about Elizabeth's growing empire, check out her blog at ReluctantLandlord.net.

Other Platforms to Consider

If you're going to list on one of these sites, you might as well cast a wide net and list on all of them. Just make sure to update your availability calendar on each platform when bookings come through.

VRBO – Vacation Rental By Owner, VRBO.com, is another marketplace for short-term vacation rentals. Janelle mentioned that nearly half of her bookings actually come from VRBO.

Home Away – HomeAway.com is a well-established vacation rental site specializing in whole-house rentals.

HouseTrip – HouseTrip.com is a European-focused, whole-home vacation rental marketplace.

FlipKey – FlipKey.com is another vacation rental site, but has the unique advantage of having listings syndicated on Tripadvisor.com, one of the most popular travel sites in the world.

CorporateHousingByOwner – As you might have guessed from the name, CorporateHousingByOwner.com is a marketplace where you can list your furnished property to corporate tenants on a short-term or long-term basis, like Elizabeth.

Roomorama – Roomorama.com is another marketplace like Airbnb.

Homestay – This platform focuses on booking stays where the homeowner is present, where most of the Airbnb stays I've booked have been for the "whole" house or apartment. When I ran a search for an upcoming trip to San Diego, I found rates from $27-65 a night.

Wimdu | 9flats – Airbnb clones with a heavier presence in Europe.

Onefinestay – Onefinestay.com is a very high-end version of Airbnb, focusing primarily on luxury vacation and short-term rentals in select markets.

Roomster | Roommates.com – These platforms specialize in finding long-term tenants for your spare room.

Flat-Club.com – This platform aims to help landlords and spare-bedroom-lords fill vacancies with "medium-term" tenants—stays from a few weeks to a few months.

Farm Stay US – If you live on a farm or ranch, FarmStayUS.com is a niche marketplace to welcome guests on your property and "restore lost connections to the land." When I searched near me in California, I found rates from $200 per night.

Vrumi | Spacehop – Both Vrumi.com and Spacehop.com let you rent out your home during the day, but not overnight. The idea is that while you're at work, the otherwise idle space could be put to use by a freelancer, small business, or startup.

Share Your Ideas

New companies are often looking for help coming up with names for their businesses or product lines. **Namestation.com** lets them crowdsource suggestions from creative people like you. According to the site, top contributors earn up to $300 a month part time.

You can also win cash prizes for your game-changing, problem-solving ideas at Innocentive.com. With millions of dollars awarded since 2008, companies, non-profits, and even government agencies are paying serious bucks. For example, NASA (yes, *that* NASA) paid $15,000 to Yury Bodrov of Russia for ideas about how to keep food fresh in space and $25,000 to Alex Altshuler of Massachusetts for help with a "microgravity laundry system."

Similarly, companies turn to Jovoto.com to solve pressing challenges in their businesses and reward "creatives"—contributors like you—for the help. The platform has paid out more than $6 million to "crowdstormers" since 2007.

Share Your Investment Strategy

Motif Investing lets you create your own mutual funds, buckets of up to 30 stocks and share them with others. When you join Motif's Creator Royalty Program, you can earn $1 for everyone else who buys your Motif.

Plus, the company will give you up to $150 just for signing up and making a few trades.

Instavest makes it easy to replicate the stock picks of pro investors. If you're an experienced investor,

Instavest.com says you can earn up to $5,000 per investment "thesis" by sharing it on the site.

Share Your Lock Screen?

The free Slidejoy app puts advertising on your phone's lock screen, and you earn money every time you unlock your phone—whether or not you engage with the ad. It won't make you rich, but could earn you an easy $5-15 a month. At press time, Slidejoy is only available on Android devices.

Share Your Love of Animals

Would you quit your 9-to-5 at Goldman Sachs to watch dogs out of your apartment?

That's exactly what Michael Lam of Queens, New York, did a couple years ago when he happened upon DogVacay.com.

The site, which launched in 2012, is often described as "Airbnb for dogs." People who want to watch dogs create profiles and set their own nightly rates, and pet owners can find local sitters with a few clicks of the mouse.

It's a win-win for everyone. The sitters are all experienced animal lovers hand-screened by the company; the pups get to stay in a cozy home while their owners are away instead of getting holed up in a kennel; and the owners can relax knowing their beloved dogs are in the best hands possible.

The platform has more than 25,000 active dog "hosts" across the US and Canada, including artists and creative freelancers looking to supplement their income, students, retirees, and even those who've turned sitting into a full-time gig.

Michael is one of the latter. He charges $60/night per dog and hosts up to 6 pups at a time (up to $360 per night!) in his Queens apartment, which he shares with his wife, Julie, and their Goldendoodle, Toby.

Michael worked as a programmer at Goldman Sachs for more than five years, but grew tired of the office politics. After he quit, he explained he planned to "either join a tech company or work on building mobile apps." It was during this period of unemployment he happened upon DogVacay.

"I decided to sign up as a host because I had lots of free time," Michael added. "And because it seemed like a great chance to get to play with dogs and get paid for it, too."

"My wife and I both love dogs, but neither of us had one growing up," he said. "I obsessively watched *The Dog Whisperer* and read Cesar Millan's books. That helped me understand dog behaviors and how they communicate."

"When we were dating, we'd literally go to the dog park to watch dogs play, hoping one would come up to us. After we moved in together, we finally got our dog, Toby. Still, the idea of getting to play with all different types of dogs was a dream come true."

When Michael decided to make hosting with DogVacay his full-time career, he went to dog trainer school to formalize his education, explaining, "When I saw the changes I was able to make in some dogs and in the lives of my clients, I really felt like I was making a difference."

He offered this advice to aspiring pet sitters: "Keep the owners updated with photos and videos. My dog guests are like children to their owners."

Marie Dolphin is a freelance photographer who supplements her income with DogVacay hosting. She charges $45 a night at her Redondo Beach, California, home.

She spoke highly of the opportunity in that "it pays the bills and allows me to work on my art. I highly recommend DogVacay for those who love animals and enjoy being able to make money from home."

On the power of the marketplace, Marie noted the convenience of having all your client communication in one place and that you don't have to ask for payment—DogVacay does that. "I see a lot of advertising for the site," she added, which means the company is spending money to attract new customers to the platform to the benefit of hosts like Marie.

The company also provides an emergency vet contact, insurance coverage, and a backup if you're unable to host. Marie explained, "I like the fact that your client won't be stranded should you get sick or injured. They're already in the DogVacay system and can be matched up with someone else based on the notes we write about our experiences with the pet."

She echoed Michael's advice of keeping owners updated with pictures, videos, and messages, and also recommended doing a meet-and-greet before accepting the hosting gig so you and the dog can feel each other out.

Other Platforms to Consider

Rover.com – Earn $20-60 a night pet sitting for others in your town. You set your own rates and availability, and Rover handles the payments and covers insurance and vet assistance.

The platform also supports dog walking and doggy day care.

Bonus: *Get $20 off your pup's first visit at sidehustlenation.com/rover.*

Pawshake – UK-based pet lovers can register as a pet sitter on Pawshake.co.uk and earn money watching their neighbors' animals.

Share Your Money

Note: I don't have an attorney, but my editor encouraged me to add the disclaimer that this section does not constitute investment advice. Proceed with caution.

Peer-to-Peer Lending

One of my first experiences with the sharing economy was when I signed up as a lender on **Prosper.com**. The platform offers peer-to-peer loans for debt consolidation, startups, weddings, and more. I've been a Prosper lender since 2011 and have earned 13.2% annualized returns over that time.

Here's how it works. You buy fractional ownership in a wide portfolio of loans, each with a minimum investment of $25. You can see what borrowers are using the money for, their credit rating, their employment status and more—before making a decision to invest.

(Or you can automate this whole process once you're comfortable with the platform.)

Each Prosper loan is assigned a letter grade A through E, with "A" and "B" notes being lower risk and lower returns and with "D" and "E" notes carrying higher risk and higher returns. My Prosper strategy has been to build a diversified portfolio of high-risk, high-return notes, and so far, it's paying off.

Prosper also offers "AA" grade loans for very well-qualified borrowers, and "HR" grade loans for extremely high-risk borrowers.

Like the other peer-to-peer platforms listed below, your cash isn't as liquid as with other, more traditional investments. (Prosper notes carry a 3- or 5-year payback term.) But my diversified portfolio of notes spins off $200-250 in cash flow every month.

The liquidity is something to keep in mind if you might need the cash in the near term. There is a secondary market where you can sell your notes before they mature, but they might not fetch full price.

The Prosper platform has experienced some impressive growth since I came on board, both in terms of the number and volume of "originations" and the number of lenders competing for the most attractive loans to lend on.

I use a third-party software tool called Lending Robot to automatically deploy idle cash, since I found that Prosper's built-in auto-investing feature wasn't firing fast enough to pick up the most attractive notes.

(Lending Robot charges a .45% management fee, but your first $10k is managed for free.)

My Lending Strategy

Because of the markedly higher returns among the lower grade notes, I've tried to skew my portfolio toward those. If E and HR notes have the best returns, why not just invest in them exclusively?

Because there aren't that many available. Or rather, there aren't that many available that *also* meet my "diamonds in the rough" criteria.

Because Prosper (and rival Lending Club) makes historical loan performance available, you can do your own analysis on what borrower criteria seem to impact the payback rates the most. This allows you to uncover the D, E, and HR loans that *historically* have performed safer than their peers, while still earning a great return.

Does the borrower credit score really matter? Income level? Employment status? Whether they're a homeowner or not?

Playing around with these different factors can be quite fascinating, and I use a site called NickelSteamroller.com to test different filtering scenarios. The reason this is important is filtering can add several percentage points to your return as opposed to just investing in loans "off the shelf."

Even if you went after lower risk loans, you could still earn a healthy 5-10%. Not a bad way to put some excess cash to use if you're looking for an alternative investment.

I invest $25-50 per loan to make sure I'm diversified on the platform and am not out too much money if any one note defaults.

Chargeoffs

Defaults, or chargeoffs, are the biggest risk of investing on Prosper. These loans are unsecured debt, meaning there's no collateral and little recourse for lenders to seek if the borrower doesn't pay it back.

The "sticker rate" on D-grade notes may be 20-24%, but a certain percentage of those will default. That's why Prosper's own published expected rate of return for those notes is 12.47%.

In total, 12.5% of my loans have defaulted, and another 5.2% of my active notes are currently delinquent.

One drawback to peer-to-peer investing is that you are limited in the amount of loan chargeoffs you can deduct from your investing income each year on your taxes. As it stands now, my understanding is that you can only claim up to $3,000 worth of chargeoffs per year.

After that, you're probably better off investing in other assets or switching to a peer-to-peer portfolio with less risky notes. The challenge is you won't know your chargeoff total until the year is over and you get your tax forms from Prosper.

Still, I'm a fan of peer lending. It's fun to be able to help people consolidate debt, start a business, or even start a family. On top of that, the double-digit returns and monthly cash flow make Prosper a welcome addition to my overall investment picture.

Other Platforms to Consider

Lending Club – LendingClub.com is the other big US peer-to-peer lending platform.

Lending Crowd | RateSetter | Zopa | QuidCycle – These are the leading peer-to-peer lending platforms in the UK, with investor rates of up to 6.5%.

ThinCats – Invest in Australian business loans on ThinCats.com and earn up to 9% returns.

Afluenta – Afluenta.com is the leading peer-lending platform in Latin America, offering investors returns of up to 45%.

Real Estate Investments

Fundrise is a crowdsourced commercial real estate investing platform with a couple "eREITs" to choose from: income and growth. Since it's open to non-accredited investors and the minimum investment is just $1,000, I decided to give it a shot. If you don't earn 15% on your money, you don't pay Fundrise.com a management fee.

GroundFloor – Investors can earn up to 12% lending on short-term real estate rehab projects. Similar to Prosper, you can buy fractional ownership (starting at just $10) of these notes to spread your risk around.

RealtyMogul | RichUncles – These newly launched eREITs allow investors to earn 6-7% dividends on a curated portfolio of income-generating commercial properties.

PeerStreet | Yieldstreet | RealtyShares | Money360 | LendingHome | Patch of Land | PeerRealty | EquityMultiple – Accredited investors can earn 10-15% returns on these crowdfunding platforms for commercial and residential real estate loans.

Invest in Startups

Kickfurther is pitched as a way for investors to help small local businesses buy inventory while earning a healthy return. According to the company's site, it's paid out more than $2.5 million, and users are averaging a 27% annualized profit.

When I spoke with members of the Kickfurther.com team, they actually shied away from "investment" terminology, instead explaining their platform as a way for consumers to "participate in retail" and earn a share of the profits. How it works is you help fund units of inventory—with no minimum purchase—and get paid back with profit when the company sells them.

Side Hustle Nation reader Jose Vieitez said he really likes the platform. "I've supported about 200 deals at this point," he explained, adding, "I found that getting 15-35% yearly return is way better than

69

leaving money in my savings account at .01% interest."

He mentioned his strategy was looking for deals with companies "that have multiple other products they sell, so that if this product slows down, they can use the revenues of other products to pay back." Even better are the ones that have a history of paying back Kickfurther loans, he added.

"You'll find companies that have robust retail distribution partnerships in place—like Target and Walmart," Jose said, indicating those are likely better bets "than companies that are more seasonal" or rely on unpredictable and expensive trade shows.

Throughout the process, brands actively communicate with buyers. If a brand is having a hard time selling the inventory, buyers can opt to take control of the units they purchased or have Kickfurther seize them and liquidate them on their behalf.

The platform is still maturing (the company was founded in 2014), but 94% of the deals have been successful so far. I'm testing this myself, as it seems like a compelling way to support promising companies and products you like while earning a positive return as well.

Other Platforms to Consider

FundersClub – FundersClub.com allows you to invest in pre-vetted startups in a sort of mini-mutual-fund way, meaning you can diversify your startup investing without the pressure of picking one moonshot winner.

The company claims that its picks earned a 37% unrealized internal rate of return over the past few years. I may have to throw a few dollars into this pot and see what happens.

Bonus: *Get $100 to seed your investing account at sidehustlenation.com/fundersclub.*

Wefunder – Invest in startups on the Wefunder.com platform, which is now open to non-accredited investors. Be prepared to potentially wait a long time to see a return, since it usually takes a public stock offering or acquisition to cash out your shares.

SeedInvest – Invest as little as $100 in pre-screened startups on SeedInvest.com.

AngelList – Accredited investors can back well-known venture capitalists and angel investors in their early stage startup investments on the high-risk, high-reward Angel.co platform.

CircleUp – CircleUp.com links accredited investors with consumer product and retail companies in need of capital. At press time, prospective and historical returns were not listed.

Crowdcube – Crowdcube.com facilitates investments in early stage British startups.

AgFunder – Accredited investors can invest in promising agriculture businesses or let AgFunder.com put together a fund of curated companies to invest in on their behalf. No prospective returns are listed, though AgFunder indicates it's raised more than $32 million from nearly 3,000 investors.

Share Your Muscles

Channel your athletic glory days and help young athletes level up their game. You can set your own rate on CoachUp.com, where private coaches report earning an average of $45 an hour.

Certified personal trainers can complete virtual training sessions on Wello.com and get paid via direct deposit. Set your own hours and availability, and take your training business from local to global.

Share Your Nerdiness

Are you the go-to guy or girl in your social circle for technical help? If so, you can earn money helping with computer setup, networking installations, TV mounting, and more from homeowners and businesses in your city.

HelloTech.com promises "tech support to your door." Earn $25 an hour making tech support, troubleshooting, and device installation house calls near you.

HelloTech is free for "geeks" to join, and you get paid directly to your bank account for each job you complete.

Other Platforms to Consider

Codementor – Share your coding expertise and earn money helping newbies on Codementor.io.

You can set your own rate, and generally I'm seeing rates around $15-30 for a 15-minute session. Knock a few out back to back, and you're at $60-120 an hour.

HourlyNerd – MBA students and graduates from select universities can apply to be an Hourly Nerd and take on projects from small businesses and corporate clients all around the world. Put that degree to use and earn $75-200 an hour on this growing platform.

Bugcrowd – By becoming a Bugcrowd.com researcher, you can earn cash prizes for uncovering security flaws or other "bugs" in the systems of top companies like Tesla, Pinterest, and Western Union. Ethical hackers are earning anywhere from $25 to $10,000 per bug they find.

Equity Directory – EquityDirectory.com is currently in invite-only beta, but the premise is this: you can work for promising startups in exchange for equity in the company. It's an interesting play for side hustlers because you can work on a project you're interested in or passionate about with the potential for a big payout down the road.

Share Your News Feed?

Are you a social media celebrity? If you have a minimum of 5,000 followers on Instagram, YouTube, Twitter, Facebook, or other social channels, FameBit.com wants to connect you with advertisers eager to get in front of your audience.

As a content creator, you can set your own sponsorship rates and only work with brands you're comfortable promoting. Deals range from $50 to $2,000 and up, depending on the size of your audience and what kind of package you can offer.

Similarly, Coopertize.com, TapInfluence, and Izea.com coordinate sponsored content for bloggers. I once earned $300 through Izea hosting a sponsored piece for E*TRADE.

Share Your Office

LiquidSpace | PivotDesk | Sharedesk | DesksNear.Me | Desktime – Rent out extra office space for 3 hours or 3 years on these platforms that aim to cut out traditional commercial leasing brokers. Naturally, rates vary market to market and could be $200 for a meeting room for a day or several thousand dollars a month for a startup team space with 10 desks.

Breather – If you have a "peaceful, practical space" to share, you can list it on Breather.com and command rates of $30-60 an hour.

Splacer – Splacer.co is a peer-to-peer platform specializing in short-term event or production rentals. If you own event space or could host a killer wedding reception in your backyard, there might be a side hustle opportunity here.

Tagvenue – In the UK, Tagvenue is the place to discover and book unique venues for parties, weddings, meetings, and more. Make money off your space by renting it out for events.

Share Your Opinion

Earn $10 for completing 20-minute online user tests of websites, apps, shopping portals, and more on UserTesting.com. Special software tracks your mouse movement while your webcam and mic record your eye movement, facial expressions, and words as you complete the questions.

You have to act fast, though, when new studies are released; in my experience UserTesting tests disappear very quickly.

Other Platforms to Consider

InboxDollars | **Swagbucks** – Don't expect to earn an amazing hourly rate, but you can earn gift cards, cash, and other rewards by answering surveys, watching videos, playing games, and shopping online with both of these sites.

<u>uTest</u> – The uTest.com platform pays testers to complete various company-sponsored projects and claims to have paid out over $20 million in 2015.

<u>Validately</u> – Earn $5 for each 5-minute "talk aloud" user study you complete.

<u>Try My UI</u> – Get paid $10 to test user interfaces for websites and apps on TryMyUI.com. A typical study takes 20 minutes.

<u>SliceThePie</u> – SliceThePie.com pays you to write reviews of new songs, fashion items, accessories, and commercials before they are released to the general public. Your reviews aren't publicized; they go directly to the artists/creatives to give them feedback.

Share Your Receipts?

The free Ibotta app pays you cash for taking pictures of your receipts from more than 80 chains, including Walmart, Safeway, Kroger, Publix, Costco, and Target.

Once you download the app, browse the listings before you go shopping to unlock cash rewards on the products you were going to buy anyway. You have to "unlock" the rebate by answering a quick question or two.

For example, the app asked me if I was going to buy Budweiser before I saw that I could get $3 back and also asked me when I last drank a Budweiser product. ("No" and "within the last 7 days," if you're curious!)

After you buy the item, you simply scan the barcode and submit a photo of your receipt. The cash will hit your Ibotta account within 48 hours. You can pull it out with PayPal or Venmo, or you can exchange it for gift cards.

Get a free $10 sign-up credit at sidehustlenation.com/ibotta.

Share Your Seat (on an Airplane)

No, you don't need to have a stranger sit on your lap! But if you've got a primo seat on your next flight, you can sell it to someone stuck in a middle seat in the back of the plane using the super-niche Seateroo.com app.

Share Your Space

If you have extra parking, why not put it to good use and get paid for it?

Anna Hamill lives near Twickenham Stadium in London, and has earned over £1700 (roughly $2,200) by renting out 3 spaces on her driveway on JustPark.com. The platform has a little more traction in the UK, but is growing in popularity in the US, thanks to its proposition of saving drivers up to 70% on their parking—while providing homeowners with extra income at the same time.

Anna's spots are about a 10-minute walk from the stadium and tend to get fully booked up whenever there is a rugby match, with fans relishing the chance to find cheap and convenient parking.

Anna, 55, charges £15 a stay, and found JustPark an easy way to bring in extra income. "I'm impressed how easy it is for us to get bookings" she said.

"Payments are made directly into my account, so it's a stress-free way of making a bit of money. I've taken my mum on a few weekends away with the earnings."

Other Platforms to Consider

ParqEx – Rent out your empty or often unused parking space(s) with ParqEx.com. You can even securely share access to garage spots with the free app.

When I spoke with Danny Weiss, the founder of ParqEx, he gave the example of a neighborhood dentist's office in Chicago. The practice had a small 3-car lot, which was rarely used by patients, who typically walk to their appointments.

The office is located in a neighborhood where parking is extremely difficult, and many commuters circle the area for 30-45 minutes looking for available public parking.

The dentist agreed to list his spots on ParqEx, and a few nearby businesses quickly became aware of the opportunity. Now, the spots are booked almost every day through the app. The dentist earns around $400/month ($4,800 annually) of passive income, and other local businesses have access to much-needed parking options.

ParqEx is currently in Chicago only, but is expanding to new markets.

Roost – Roost.com is the peer-to-peer marketplace for extra storage and parking spaces. "Turn your attic into extra cash."

Spacii – The Spacii.co platform connects people who have extra stuff to store with those who have extra space. If you've got some excess storage capacity, list your space here to fill it and get paid.

StoreNextDoor | **Storemates** – In the UK, use StoreNextDoor.com or Storemates.co.uk to find renters who want to store stuff in your spare bedroom or attic.

StoreX – StoreX.me is another startup aiming to disrupt the traditional self-storage industry. Earn money by listing your extra space and hosting other people's stuff.

Share Your Stuff

Earn money renting out all of the seldom-used stuff you have lying around, such as lawn mowers, tents, ladders, volleyball nets, KitchenAid mixers, etc., on NeighborGoods.net.

Nearby I found an Xbox 360 for $25 a day, a chainsaw for $41 a day, and a Louis Vuitton handbag for $31.25 a day. Definitely a wide variety of listings!

I connected briefly with Shreyans Parekh, a product manager for a tech company in the San Francisco Bay Area. "I have rented numerous products on

NeighborGoods, including power tools, my bicycle, and old toys," he explained. "I typically earn $75-150 per month renting my products on the site."

Other Platforms to Consider

Spinlister – Rent out your "ride" on Spinlister.com—your bike, your skis or snowboard, or surfboard.

I found bikes listed in San Francisco from $25-70 per day, and thought it was nice that they listed the appropriate rider height fit, so I could filter out the ones that were too small.

Open Shed – In Australia, OpenShed.com.au's users can earn "pocket money" renting out their seldom-used items to friends and neighbors.

UseTwice – UseTwice.at is a peer-to-peer rental platform for household tools and goods in Germany.

PlanetReuse.com – Sell used building materials on this environmentally friendly, specialty marketplace.

Share Your Support

Become a Crowdio customer service agent and get paid for every live chat interaction you resolve. Crowdio supplies the customers, and all you have to do is take good care of them.

Denmark-based Crowdio calls this "the world's best part-time job" because you choose your own hours, can work from anywhere in the world, and can opt to work only with the companies and websites that interest you.

When I reached out to the team members behind Crowdio, they sent me a couple examples of people using their platform as support agents.

The first is Enver, who fell in love and married a Turkish woman. Due to harsh immigration laws, he was not allowed to bring her and their children back to his home in Denmark. Discouraged but not defeated, he set out to find online work he could complete from Turkey and came across Crowdio.com. Today, he uses the platform in combination with other freelance work to support his family.

Martin didn't quite suffer from the same geopolitical circumstances, but saved up his Crowdio earnings to move to Barcelona. He still works on the platform today, earning a "very decent living" in a location-independent manner.

Share Your Time

In-Person and Virtual Assistant Platforms

Earn $25-200 to go look at stuff like eBay purchases, cars, rental properties, or even vacant lots with WeGoLook.com. Take pictures, verify listing information, and report back what you find.

Alfred – Visit HelloAlfred.com to sign on as a professional "Alfred"—a modern day urban butler sold on a subscription-membership model—and get paid to run errands for busy clients.

Fun fact: the company gets its name from Batman's butler.

Luxe – Luxe.com is an on-demand valet parking service available in select cities that often costs less than parking at your destination. Valets earn money by meeting customers, taking their cars and keys, and then reuniting with them later upon request.

Fancy Hands | Zirtual | Time Etc | eaHELP | HireMyMom.com | VirtualAssistantJobs.com – These are just a handful of the virtual assistant companies that hire part-time remote workers. Pay generally ranges from $10-20 an hour.

Mystery Shopping Apps

Download the free Field Agent app to find top-secret tasks nearby, like checking a store for certain products, photographing a display, or asking a store employee a question. Each task pays $3-12 and is relatively quick to complete if you're in the neighborhood already.

Gigwalk – Become a Gigwalker and look for similar in-person "gigs" that can generally be completed in just a few minutes with your smartphone.

Mobee | EasyShift | Rewardable – This trio of mystery-shopping apps offers small payouts for completing quick questionnaires while you run errands.

Streetspotr – Perform market-research tasks with this UK-based app and earn "serious pocket money."

QuickThoughts – Download the free QuickThoughts app to access paid surveys and "missions" based on your location, such as taking pictures of product displays at stores. Payouts generally range from $1-3 per survey, and you'll get $0.10 for completing each screener questionnaire even if you don't qualify.

Micro-Task Platforms

Micro-Task Platforms pay you a small fee ($0.01 to $3) for each mini-job you complete. Tasks might include answering a brief survey, identifying what's in a picture, or proofreading a block of text.

Over the past couple of years, Mike Naab has earned over $21,000 in his spare time completing surveys and other small jobs on **Mechanical Turk**, the most popular micro-task platform.

Mike is an analyst, writer, and online entrepreneur who's turned his free time into an extra $150-300 per week. He blogs at TopMoneyHabits.com.

Mike came across the mturk.com site when he was looking for a side hustle right before his first daughter was born. "I was putting together a mental checklist of all the expenses we were about to incur: daycare, diapers, food, etc., and I started freaking out a little bit," he explained.

He wanted something he could do from home to supplement his income, since both he and his wife were working full time. "The last thing I wanted to do when starting a family was to pick up a part-time job and never be home," Mike told me. "So I started looking to see if I could find a way to make money online."

He said he went down a rabbit hole of ways to make money online from home, and mostly found a bunch of scams or low-paying survey sites that paid in gift cards instead of cash.

Finally, he came across a list of money-making ideas that mentioned Amazon Mechanical Turk, a site where businesses, researchers, universities, and consumer product groups post tasks to be completed by online workers. While normally skeptical, Mike said, "I figured since it was owned by Amazon, it was probably legit."

The platform is legit—I've actually used it as a buyer myself to get some tedious data entry work done, but never considered using it as a worker. Mike decided to give it a shot.

The tasks on Amazon Mechanical Turk are called HITs, or human intelligence tasks, which are posted by people called "requesters."

Each HIT lists the payment and the timeframe for completing the task. You can scroll through the list of work available (typically hundreds of thousands of HITs at any given time) and accept the ones you want to work on. Once you complete the work, you submit the HIT and await payment.

Mike explained, "There are a large variety of HITs available to work on. Surveys are probably the most common type of HIT with topics ranging from consumer products, personality, finance, ethics, education, etc."

If surveys aren't your thing, there are also audio/video transcriptions, categorization tasks, Excel spreadsheet work, YouTube video ratings, and more.

I was skeptical that anyone could make real money on this platform, and asked Mike for his take. "Your potential earnings really depend on how much time you put into it," he said. "I typically make anywhere from $150-300/week and have earned over $21,000 in total by doing nothing but working on tasks right from my computer at home."

He added that while there's work available immediately upon signing up, many of the higher paying requesters require you to complete a certain number of HITs before you can work on their tasks. Mike said that qualifications of 100/500/1,000 HITs completed are pretty common to access some of the better work on there.

In that sense, it's similar to other freelance platforms where you might have to "put in your time" with some lower paying work in order to build up your portfolio.

Having worked on Amazon Mechanical Turk for 2.5 years completely as a side hustle, Mike has completed more than 87,000 HITs. As far as income, that averages out to $0.24 per task, which might not seem like much, but has definitely added up over time to some significant earnings.

So what about those who are just starting out without all of those HITs completed?

"I've gotten a few friends of mine signed up and earning $100/week after only a couple of weeks," he said. "I try to look at it from an hourly rate standpoint. Sure, a survey might only give you $0.40, but it might take you 2 minutes to finish. That's a $12/hour pay rate, and you made it sitting on your computer at home."

Every HIT is going to be a different pay rate (since each comes from a different requester), but Mike explained you can probably expect to average $6-12/hour.

"Some HITs are amazing," he added. "I've had $3 surveys that took me 2 minutes (a $90/hour rate!) and batches of work that are 25 cents each but I could complete 3-4 per minute. It's just a matter of being on there at the right time."

One thing to consider with Mechanical Turk is the opportunity cost. We're talking about less than minimum wage in some cases. Is there another activity that would bring you more fulfillment or income?

Admittedly, I delegated work there because it was cheap labor that didn't require any specialized skills. If you think your time is worth more per hour, you're probably right; it's just a matter of finding a client with a problem you can solve.

Still, Mechanical Turk represents an easy-to-start side hustle, and you can see some results with it right away, even if the initial dollar figures aren't huge. Persistence pays, and as Mike has shown, the quarters *do* add up.

"What I love about it is the flexibility," he told me. "You can work on there all day or for 10 minutes, if you have a break in your day."

You can transfer your earnings directly into your bank account or spend it like cash on Amazon. There's also no minimum to hit before you cash out (unlike some other survey sites).

Mike went on to explain that while Amazon Mechanical Turk is convenient, it's not perfect. (No platform is.)

He said the highest paying work tends to come during normal working hours on weekdays. "If you only have time to do it at nights or on weekends, you'll still find work, but likely not as much good work," he explained.

"It's also not going to make you rich," he added. "The pay is pretty decent, but it definitely works better as a supplemental source of income."

Additionally, he mentioned that there is work available in most countries, but only workers in the US and India can withdraw cash. Workers from other countries can only redeem their earnings through Amazon gift cards.

New users can sign up for free at mturk.com. Mike said it takes about 48 hours to approve your account and verify your social security number for tax purposes.

Once verified, you start out in a probation period where you need to complete at least one HIT for 10 days. During that period, you have a cap of 100 HITs per day, and you can't withdraw your money. After the 10 days are over, there are no withdrawal restrictions.

Other Platforms to Consider

Crowdflower – Join 1.5 million global contributors completing small data entry jobs for big companies on Crowdflower.com. You decide how much or how little to work on the platform.

Microworkers | **ShortTask** – These platforms are similar to Mechanical Turk (above), but with a smaller task selection.

Share Your Travel Savvy

FlightFox is a unique human-powered flight search engine. In fact, it guarantees it can save you money on your next flight, or you'll get your money back. (I'm definitely going to put it to the test on my next international trip!)

But it needs sophisticated travel-hacking experts to run queries and build itineraries for clients. If you have a knack for saving money on flights, apply to join this network of part-time, flight-booking gurus.

Share Your Truck

If you have a truck or van—and a strong back—you can earn money on **Dolly.com**'s peer-to-peer moving platform. Help your neighbors pack and move across town.

Other Platforms to Consider

Buddytruk – Earn up to $40 an hour helping neighbors pack and move across town on the Buddytruk.com platform. You bring the truck and work together to get the job done.

GoShare – Put your truck or cargo van to work helping people move and earn up to $62 an hour on GoShare.co.

uShip – If you're making a long road trip, you might as well take a look and see if someone on uShip.com needs to move or send something to where you're headed. Rates vary based on the size and weight of the items, along with the distance of the journey.

Share Your Yard

If having guests in your home Airbnb-style makes you a little uncomfortable, how would you feel about them staying in your yard? With Camp In My Garden you can turn your backyard into a mini-campground and earn $10-30 per person per night.

> *Bonus:* This section covered dozens of sharing economy marketplaces, many of which have special sign-up offers if you want to try them out yourself. I should note that most of these offers are for joining the "buyer" side of the platform, but will help you save money either way.
>
> Download the free list of $1150 in Sharing Economy discounts and credits at BuyButtonsBook.com/bonus.

Downsides to the Sharing Economy

"Sharing is sometimes more demanding than giving."

—Mary Catherine Bateson

The sharing economy is not without its detractors and naysayers. For consumers, these apps have unlocked a world of convenience and cost savings, but for sharing economy workers and other stakeholders, the picture isn't always so rosy.

Platform Risk

The first risk is one that you'll always have to be aware of when building your business on the back of a third-party platform. What happens if that platform goes out of business? Or gets acquired? Or changes its rules?

I call these "platform risk" factors, and the bad news is they are largely beyond your control. In late 2015, the third-largest ridesharing platform, Sidecar, shut its doors.

Naturally, the more established and well-funded a platform is, the lower the risk that it will go out of business, but you never know when the rules—or the pay rate—may change.

Uber is notoriously cutthroat about this, having slashed its rates several times over the past few years. Each time, drivers are left in a take-it-or-leave-it position: they can either keep driving and accept the lower payouts, or they can hang up their keys and decide it's no longer worth their time. Ultimately, Uber may remove drivers from the equation altogether; the company tested its first fleet of driverless cars in 2016.

To mitigate your risk, try to diversify your income streams by setting up shop on as many similar marketplaces as makes sense. Also, consider how you might build your own standalone brand and service.

Regulatory Risk

The next big area of concern when it comes to the sharing economy is legal and regulatory risk. Some platforms operate in a legal gray area, and it may be years before our laws catch up with the market.

In New York City, a report found that 56% of the city's 51,000 Airbnb listings "illegally offered to book an entire apartment or home for fewer than 30 days." So far, lawmakers haven't done much to enforce any penalties, but the risk is there.

In Montreal, the city declared Uber illegal and seized 400 driver-owned vehicles. Uber ended up paying the impound fees and offered loaner cars to its drivers, but no doubt it was a scary and intimidating experience for everyone involved.

To mitigate your regulatory risk, check with your local city and state rules, consult with other sellers in your area, and stay within the guidelines of the sharing economy platform you're working on.

Health Insurance and Other Benefits

For workers who want to become full-time freelancers or sharing economy workers, the question of health insurance always comes up. In the US, where health insurance is usually tied to employment, this is a big monthly expense you need to budget for if you break out on your own full time.

Uber and other platforms maintain that their workers are independent contractors, not employees. This keeps costs low for the company and for consumers, but shifts the burden of buying health insurance, saving for retirement, and paying estimated taxes on to you, the worker.

Societal Disruptions

Around the turn of the 20th century, an Austrian economist named Joseph Schumpeter coined the term "Creative Destruction." What he meant was that sometimes when we create new value, old value gets destroyed. And while that may sound harsh, it describes what many sharing economy platforms do. They remove traditional intermediaries, gatekeepers, and established service providers.

For example, taxi use in San Francisco is down 65% following the rise of Uber and Lyft. Because of Airbnb, the traditional rental market is feeling a pinch in many popular tourist cities because landlords can earn more on short-term rentals than on traditional 12-month leases.

The combined effect of millions of these sharing economy transactions is long-running companies going out of business and hard-working people losing their jobs.

Is It Worth It?

The sharing economy presents a new and novel way to earn extra money outside of your day job, but be aware of your true hourly wage. I recommend tracking your time and calculating how much you're really bringing home after expenses and taxes.

The number might be quite a bit lower than the "sticker price" hourly rate advertised, and you'll have to ask yourself if it's worth it. If you find a platform with the opportunity for growth where the work is fun, by all means, stick with it. But if you come to dread the work and the income doesn't justify your input, move on.

The other thing to consider with many sharing economy platforms is you don't always have the power to charge what you're worth. When you're just another cog in the system and anyone can provide the service to the same ability you can, rates are naturally going to gravitate downward. The platforms I'm most excited about are the ones where you have an opportunity to differentiate yourself with the quality of your service or your unique personality and skills.

In the next section, I'll show you some unique marketplaces to put your individual talents, skills, and experience to use.

Marketplaces to Sell Your Skills

"A winner is someone who recognizes his talents, works his tail off to develop them into skills, and uses these skills to accomplish his goals."

—Larry Bird

While the sharing economy is a great place to start, you'll always be able to earn more by selling something highly specialized. For example, I've met website designers who charge $20,000 or more for custom-built websites. I've met writers who charge $10,000 or more for custom copywriting packages. I've met photographers who charge $3,000 or more for taking pictures.

And that's why sharing economy apps that have you take surveys or deliver groceries all gravitate toward a low hourly rate. If anyone can do it and there aren't any special skills involved, it's probably not going to make you rich.

In this section, I'm going to help you identify the skills, talents, and experiences you have that other people and businesses might pay you for. Now, if you're like me, it might take a little convincing that you—yes, *you*—do have valuable skills.

For starters, my friend Daniel DiPiazza likes to point out that, by definition, if you've ever had a job, you had at least one skill *someone* thought was worth paying for. So when taking inventory of your skills, your résumé is one place to start. Next, I'd consider your hobbies and interests outside of work.

Like many of the successful Buy Button entrepreneurs you'll meet in this section, most of the skills I use today are entirely self-taught. I've certainly never had a job that paid me to write books or produce an online radio show!

The niche marketplaces where you can sell your skills are almost as far-reaching as those we discovered in the sharing economy, and they typically give you more control over pricing and more opportunity to differentiate yourself. On top of that, these platforms represent an excellent way to land your first customers, or if you already have a business, they can help you generate incremental revenue and diversify your income.

What can you sell? Let's dive in and find out.

Sell Your Artistic Talent

Let others discover (and hopefully buy!) your art on the free-to-join Artsicle.com marketplace.

TurningArt.com is a unique art rental marketplace for homeowners and workplaces. Artists earn royalties each time their work is rented or when prints or originals are sold through the site.

Similarly, talented emerging and established artists can apply to sell their work on RiseArt.com.

Sell Your Creations

Envato.com is a broad family of brands that connects creators of digital assets with those who need them. If you can create website templates, WordPress plugins, stock videos, jingles, graphics, and even 3D models, this is the place for you.

Sell Your Designs

Anand Thangavel is a self-taught graphic designer in the UK. In 5 years, he's earned more than $1.1 million on the freelance crowdsourced design marketplace DesignCrowd.com.

How it works is clients submit their requests—for websites, logos, business cards, etc.—and a global workforce of designers begin sending in their concepts and ideas. It's usually a winner-take-all system: the client chooses the preferred design, and then the designer gets paid.

Anand began submitting designs as a side hustle, and after winning several contests, he decided to quit his job to pursue DesignCrowd full time. He's understandably proud of hitting the $1 million mark, but noted it was the result of "thousands of jobs, sleepless nights, and continual determination."

Still, he is excited to have seen his hustle pay off and to have the flexibility to work when he likes. "Getting to this stage in my life wasn't easy, but it was worth the hard work," he said, adding that the performance-based nature of the platform gave him even more incentive to hone his skills and try to impress every client.

For new designers starting on the platform, he gave this advice:

1. Read the client's brief in detail and make sure you follow the brief closely in all your design submissions.
2. Pick colors and fonts appropriate to the client's industry and consistent with the client's website.
3. Prioritize client feedback—when a client gives feedback, focus on that first rather than working on other projects/designs.

Bonus: *Get up to $100 off your next design project at designcrowd.com/hustle.*

Nicky Laatz is a graphic designer in South Africa and one of the top-performing shop owners on CreativeMarket.com, which specializes in selling digital assets like designs, website themes, fonts, and photography.

When Nicky joined the marketplace, she was still primarily focused on one-on-one client work, but was looking for a way for her art to reach more people. "I believe every artist should find a balance between making art for others (usually according to a brief with restrictions) and making art as you want it to be," she explained. "So often, the latter ends up discarded or stored away in a dusty box. Why not try putting it up for sale? If you like it, others might enjoy it too!"

The decision to put her art up for sale turned out to be a very fruitful one, as Nicky has sold more than $1 million worth of her designs on Creative Market since 2012.

Other Platforms to Consider

99designs – 99designs.com is a well-known crowdsourcing marketplace for graphic design. If you're a talented designer with a competitive streak, you can enter design contests here and win cash prizes if your design is chosen.

ZillionDesigns – If 99 designs aren't enough, ZillionDesigns.com has you covered and offers a similar design crowdsourcing service.

Crowdspring – In addition to graphic and web design contests, Crowdspring.com also supports business-naming contests, product naming, taglines, and marketing-copy competitions. Creatives keep 100% of their winnings.

GraphicRiver – Sell your web graphics, fonts, icons, logos, and even PowerPoint presentation templates on GraphicRiver.net.

Sell Your Eagle Eye

Scribendi.com hires proofreaders and editors to work remotely and correct client documents.

Sell Your Expertise

The Expert Institute connects subject matter experts (you!) with attorneys and corporations who happily pay for your analysis and opinions.

Create an account on PopExpert.com to provide live one-on-one coaching and advice on whatever topic(s) you're qualified to assist with. The platform seems oriented toward health, wellness, and mindfulness, but has experts in other areas as well.

Set your own rates and conduct virtual sessions from your home or office at your convenience.

Sell Your Healing Touch

Zeel is the Uber for massages. Licensed masseuses can fill their unbooked time on Zeel.com and set their own schedules. Therapists earn 75% of the sticker price (around $99 for a 60-minute massage), plus an automatic 18% gratuity.

Soothe operates similarly, sending licensed massage therapists directly to the customers who request them. According to the website, Soothe.com's therapists earn 2-3x more than they would at a traditional spa and have more flexible work hours.

Bonus: *Get $30 off your first massage at sidehustlenation.com/soothe.*

Sell Your Knowledge

Online education is already a $100 billion industry, and what's exciting is that a big portion of the pie goes to individual instructors like you and me. After all, whether it's in a traditional classroom or in front of a computer screen, learning relies on great teachers. Today, a growing number of online education platforms invite you to set up your own virtual classes and get paid to teach what you know.

The largest of these marketplaces is Udemy.com. On Udemy you can create a video course in your area of expertise, set your own price (up to $200), and put it up for sale on Udemy's platform of more than 12 million students.

I've earned over $11,000 as a Udemy instructor since late 2014, and despite some recent pricing and promotion changes, I still think it is a worthwhile platform to learn about and consider putting your Buy Button on.

Although I now earn a nice, relatively passive income stream from Udemy, my first attempt at a course was a disaster. That course taught students how to hire and work with virtual assistants; it took me several weeks to create, and I barely made any sales.

After speaking with several successful instructors, I decided to take another crack at it and did much better the second time around. That second course, on how to launch a Kindle book, earned $3525 in its first 60 days and has gone on to earn money every month since. I'll explain below what I did to create and launch it on Udemy.

My Course Idea

After the successful launch of my last book, *Work Smarter*, I wrote a blog post providing a detailed, step-by-step case study of everything I did to create, launch, and market the title. A few people even joked in the comments that it should have been a book all on its own.

I then helped a few friends with their launches, and they enjoyed similar (or even greater) successes. This further validated my approach and my sense that Kindle was a hot topic. It was clear that people were actively seeking information on how to rock their launches.

I attribute part of my second course's success to the topic: many more people want to know how to launch a Kindle book than how to hire a virtual assistant. In my experience, the overall interest in a topic significantly affects a course's success or failure.

Why Udemy?

Like other Buy Button platforms listed in this book, Udemy is a marketplace of buyers—a reported 12 million students according to the Udemy.com website.

Udemy also makes it really easy for new instructors. You don't have to worry about setting up a membership login area of your site, getting special video hosting, or deciding on a payment processor.

You outline your course and then film and upload the modules. Then Udemy creates a nice-looking, conversion-optimized sales page on your behalf. Udemy also enables you to send bulk and individual messages to students in your course. You don't get students' email addresses, but you can still communicate with them.

(In many cases, students have it set up so messages or course announcements ping their inbox anyway.)

For sales you refer, you keep 97% of the revenue.

Udemy Disadvantages

Of course, when you're using someone else's platform for free, there's always going to be a cost somewhere. With Udemy, that cost comes into play when you are *not* the referrer of the student. When Udemy or one of its affiliate partners makes a sale, you only earn 25-50%.

I was OK with that because I figured those would be "gravy" sales—students that I wouldn't have reached without Udemy's help, anyway.

The other drawback to Udemy is that it caps how much you can charge for your course at $200. If you have some truly premium content, it might not make sense to part with it for such a low price. Alternatively, you could break it up into multiple courses, like Kindle Launch 101, 201, 301, etc.

Udemy also relies on frequent and steep discounting to drive sales, which can cut into your margins and potentially cheapen your brand and your content.

Despite all this, I reasoned that the pros outweighed the cons, and I wanted to take another crack at Udemy. The alternative would have been self-hosting the course, in which case I'd be responsible for *all* the marketing and technical aspects of it.

Down the road, you still own the content, and you're free to syndicate it to other online education platforms or your own website.

Pre-Launch: Outlining the Material

The first step was to outline the content. What would the course cover?

I broke down the book launch process in roughly chronological order and ended up with a really detailed 8-page outline.

Then, I went through and identified which sections would be screen recordings and which would be "talking head" sections, with me speaking directly to the camera.

In total I had around 30 different "segments," varying between 30 seconds and 10 minutes in length. On Udemy, the shorter your segments, the more engagement you'll have in your course.

For the "talking head" segments, I created a rough script of bullet points to use because I'm not the kind of person who can just turn on the camera and talk coherently. I actually printed these out and taped them to the camera. I called it my poor man's teleprompter.

The downside is that this ultimately created more editing and uploading work... more on that in a moment.

Shooting the Course

For Udemy (and other online education platforms), video is the preferred delivery medium for your content. Each Udemy course must have a minimum of 30 minutes of video content.

The good news is that if you're camera shy, you don't have to be in front of the camera that whole time. You can use screen recordings, like talking over a screen-capture or a PowerPoint presentation, if you'd like.

Since I wanted my course to have some variety, I used a combination of "talking head" videos and screen recordings.

Screen Recordings

The screen recordings were a piece of cake. I actually scripted or added to my outline for many of those, and could scroll along on my iPad while doing the demo on my laptop and recording the screen.

I batch processed these and could knock out several in one sitting. I didn't necessarily go in chronological order for the course, but jumped around and crossed them off my list as they were done.

Talking Head Videos

The talking head segments were another story completely. I tried a similar batch-processing method, but they were *much* slower.

One of the most surprising time-sucks in the recording process was how long it took to add each file to the editing software. I used the free built-in Windows Live Movie Maker software, and it was *really* slow to import and export these big movie files.

Between the equipment set-up, microphone issues, processing time, re-shoots of blurry videos, and editing, it probably wouldn't be an exaggeration to say it took an hour to produce every 5 minutes of talking head video.

In total, I ended up with around 3.5 hours of video material for the course.

Uploading to Udemy

Once I finished creating all the course material, it was time to upload to Udemy. This is a straightforward process and probably one of the biggest advantages of its platform.

Naming the Course

Udemy, like many of the other platforms mentioned in this book, is a search engine. That means it's important to include your target keywords in your course title—in my case, "kindle launch."

Rob Cubbon, a successful Udemy instructor, told me that top-selling courses offer some concrete benefit to the user, so I added in the "result" of the course: "Publish and Market an Amazon bestseller."

Editorial Review

Udemy strongly encourages new instructors to upload a test video *before* recording their entire course. That way instructors can find out if there are any video or sound issues *before* they invest several weeks in their courses—only to create something that isn't up to Udemy's standards.

After you upload all your videos and hit publish, the Udemy editorial team will give your course a once-over and make suggestions (or requirements) for improvement before it goes live on the site.

In my case, I had to remove the text from my course "cover image" and add descriptions to some of the lectures. The team recommended several other changes, but none that prevented the course from going live.

Building Social Proof

One of the biggest advantages of Udemy is that it provides an excellent conversion-optimized sales page for you. You just have to fill in your course information and gather some initial social proof.

Social proof on Udemy comes in two flavors: enrollments and reviews.

According to Scott Britton, another successful instructor, the magic numbers are 10+ reviews and 1,000+ enrollments.

These are important because they are prominently featured on the course landing pages and in Udemy's search results.

Naturally, prospective students understand there's safety in numbers. The more students and positive reviews you have, the more likely they are to invest in your course.

Thankfully, I was able to get my 10+ reviews by giving access to the course to volunteers from my email list and asking them to leave a review.

I'm confident you know 10 people who'd be willing to help you out by checking out your course and leaving a nice review.

To get the enrollments, I created a free coupon code and posted it to the Udemy Studio Facebook group, a place where Udemy instructors can solicit enrollments and feedback.

Before long, someone else had posted it on a deals site, and I started to get the requisite flood of enrollments. It felt a little weird to be giving the thing away for free just for the sake of numbers, but the truth is the *vast* majority of these freebie-seekers never even looked at the course.

Once I had my 1,000+ students, I killed the freebie offer.

My Course Launch

When I was ready to go live to the world, I posted about the course on my blog and sent out an email to my subscribers a few days later.

Now if you're thinking, "That's not fair! I don't have a blog or email list!", it might be comforting to hear that my direct efforts only accounted for $624—or 17%—of the overall launch income.

Recruiting Affiliates

The single most effective marketing tactic was finding relevant affiliates.

In fact, the affiliate channel accounted for $1801—or just over 50%—of the launch earnings.

So what makes a good affiliate? Someone with an audience you can help and who doesn't have a competing product.

For me, that was Steve Scott from SteveScottSite.com and Spencer Haws from NichePursuits.com.

On Steve's site, I had written a case study of my book launch as a guest post, which had done really well. So I gave Steve free access to the course once it was ready. Since he thought it was well done, he sent an email promoting it to his list.

With Spencer, I knew he and his team were working on a Kindle book for their authority site, so I offered them help with the launch and gave them access to the course. They ended up crushing their launch and gave me and the course a generous shout-out in their recap case study post.

In each case, I created a special coupon link for their audiences and saw really strong results.

I had a few other affiliates as well, but not everyone promoted the course—and that's OK. It's about casting a wide net to give yourself the best opportunity and to give your affiliates the best chance to serve their audiences.

I think this strategy can be used for courses in just about any industry.

Udemy's affiliate program is through LinkShare. Affiliates earn 40-50% of the sale, and the instructor earns 25%.

Fueling Ongoing Sales

Just like some of these other platforms, it's your job to provide the initial marketing push to get noticed on the platform. After that, the internal ranking algorithms and recommendation engines start to work on your behalf, and you can see additional "organic" sales from Udemy's 12 million customers.

At least that's the idea.

The Power of the Marketplace

During the 60-day launch period, I earned $1099.70 in sales from Udemy's efforts, or around 31% of the total earnings.

On the positive side, every dollar the course generates now is incremental passive income. Occasionally I'll add new content or respond to student questions, but the course is out there as an asset for me now.

Is it Really Passive Income?

All told, I usually spend less than 10 minutes a week on Udemy. One thing I like to do is send every new student a personalized welcome message on the Udemy platform. I go in once a week, and it goes pretty quickly because I have a template that I can just copy and paste.

I make sure to mention the name of the course because students often enroll in several courses and might not recognize my name. In my case, I thank them for joining me in the course, invite them to reach out if they have any questions, and ask what their book is about. I also include a link to SideHustleNation.com in my signature.

(Udemy is pretty strict about external linking, but here's a soft way to expose people to your brand and website that's perfectly legal.)

This tactic shows students I'm a real person and I believe it helps generate more positive reviews.

As a Udemy instructor, you can also send educational announcements and other interesting content to your students.

I send course announcements when I have content students might find relevant, especially Kindle-related stuff. For instance, I sent a note about my interview with Nick Stephenson, who explained how to build an email list off of Amazon book sales, and one about my conversation with Chandler Bolt, who detailed his rapid book-writing process.

I think it's a great way to drive traffic and engagement back to your site. Under Udemy's rules for educational announcements, you can't link to paid products, only to pages with additional free educational material. You can link to other Udemy courses with a promotional announcement. (There's a limit to how many promotions you can send each month.)

The Next Level: Earning a Full-Time Income Teaching Online

Phil Ebiner had never heard of passive income or online education before coming across Udemy. Having studied video creation in college, he decided to make a course and upload it to Udemy while still working a full-time job. He made $62 in his first month and was hooked.

He's since turned his part-time online teaching side hustle into a 6-figure business, and he's quit his job to focus on it full time.

His first course was on video editing and using Final Cut Pro 7. Final Cut Pro 7 has since been discontinued, which taught Phil a valuable lesson: if you want extended passive income, try to build courses around evergreen content.

When we spoke, Phil had published 52 courses and enrolled over 130,000 students. Phil is one of

Udemy's most prominent instructors and is now building his own direct sales channel at VideoSchoolOnline.com. As his audience grows, he's also finding success with YouTube, affiliate marketing, and Kindle books.

The most successful instructors I see on Udemy seem to view it as a portfolio-driven platform, meaning they're continually creating new courses.

The more excellent material you have out there, the more likely you are to be discovered and make sales.

Coming Up With Course Ideas

Phil pointed out that you don't need to be a leading expert in a field to release a training course on the subject. You just need to know more than the people learning from the course and to be able to provide clear and quality content.

For example, Phil had already studied video editing and photography, so he had a good knowledge base in those subjects. He strongly advised picking something you enjoy and are passionate about, without worrying about the income at first. He explained, "Trying to produce courses on subjects you are not interested in will set you up to fail."

Using the Udemy Platform to Your Advantage

Phil credited much of his success to leveraging the existing user base on Udemy.

When he started out, he put a lot of time and effort into building up his student base and improving his rank within Udemy. He did this with the following methods:

- Giving away free coupons.
- Giving parts of his paid courses away for free.
- Asking friends and family to buy and rate his courses.

I asked Phil if Udemy's discount promotions bothered him, but he indicated those had driven tens of thousands of new students to his courses, whom he could now message and promote other material to.

How Hard is it for New Instructors to Make Money on Udemy?

Phil told me there are around 19,000 instructors and 40,000 courses on Udemy, which "might seem crowded, but I see new instructors starting on the platform all the time and doing better than I did when I was starting out."

Phil added that while previous teaching experience isn't necessary for becoming a Udemy instructor, having some technical skills, such as his video editing experience, does come in handy. "The technical side of recording, editing, and uploading a course is where most people get bogged down," he explained.

Phil and I both use the Logitech c920, which is a great little camera. It captures good audio, and with some natural light in front of you, the picture is more than good enough. It's only around $70, so you don't need expensive equipment or artificial lighting to record good videos.

For high quality screen recordings, Phil recommended Screenflow for Mac or Camtasia for PC.

How to Build a Course

As you can imagine, with so many courses under his belt, Phil has developed a blueprint for building his courses. The most important lesson he has learned is to make sure the first few lessons are action packed with the important content. Sadly, most students will not complete your course, so grabbing their attention early is vitally important.

Put all of your best content in the first 2-5 videos. Phil starts with a short introduction as video #1, and then includes his top 5 tips for the topic in video #2. This maximizes user interest and increases the chance of the user leaving a review.

The Risk of Using a Third-Party Platform

Using Udemy and leveraging the huge audience on its platform is all well and good, unless it comes to an end. Phil found this out when a similar site called Skillfeed closed its doors. He was earning over $1,000 a month on Skillfeed and didn't expect it to shut down so suddenly. Udemy is a much bigger company and certainly does not look like it will close anytime soon, but keep this risk in mind when choosing a third-party platform to host your content.

Udemy doesn't really allow you to build your own mailing list, but it does allow a cool hack called "The Bonus Lecture," which you can tack on to the end of your courses. It can just be a PDF file that invites students to take some call to action, like visiting your website, if they enjoyed the course and want to connect with you further.

Phil has started hosting some of his courses on his own site, VideoSchoolOnline.com, and has earned some revenue as his organic presence in the search engines increases. He's also building his email list through his own site, so he can mail out information on any new courses he releases.

Advice for New and Established Instructors

I asked Phil what advice he would give new instructors to help them get the best possible start with Udemy. For new instructors with no students and no audience, this was the roadmap he suggested:

1. Put together a premium paid course around 2-3 hours in length.
2. Create a shorter free version around 30 minutes in length.
3. Promote the paid course with 500-1,000 coupons on forums and social media.
4. Work hard for that initial traction and those first students.
5. After a couple of weeks ask students to leave a review.

6. Start your own website and publish content on other platforms like YouTube.
7. Add a bonus lecture to your free course, promoting your paid course.

For instructors who already have an email list or customer base, he suggested following most of the outline above, but using your email list and/or Udemy's internal announcement tools to help promote your course at a limited time introductory price ($19-29).

What could you teach?

Other Platforms to Consider

Skillshare – I've syndicated my courses to Skillshare.com, where they don't earn as much as Udemy but still bring in some incremental passive income.

Curious.com – Curious.com is a growing online education community where members pay a monthly fee for access to a curated library of courses. If you have a lesson to share or expertise in a certain area, you can apply to teach on the platform. You earn royalties when your videos are viewed, as well as referral bonuses for generating new student sign-ups.

Pluralsight – Pluralsight.com specializes in corporate education and ongoing training in specific technical and creative areas, such as software programming and graphic design. When you apply to be a course author on this platform, you can earn royalties based on how many times your videos are viewed.

Coursmos – Coursmos.com is an online education platform where you can set your own prices for your course without any limits.

RocketLearn | 360Training | Eliademy – These are other online course platforms where you can syndicate your lessons.

Lynda – If you are a "top professional" in your field, you can apply to teach on Lynda.com, a popular online education community owned by LinkedIn.

> **Bonus:** Want to learn more about teaching online? Grab the free Online Teaching bonus at BuyButtonsBook.com/bonus.
>
> Inside you'll find a step-by-step methodology to validate your course idea and learn how to sell it to eager students on your own platform.

Sell Your Language Skills

Chad Hansen began teaching English on Verbling.com in 2013, and has since logged thousands of lessons and earned more than $100,000 on the platform. He said he loves being able to support his family working online and set his own schedule. "I teach amazing, uplifting, positive, forward-thinking people from all over the world," Chad explained.

Verbling turned out to be a savior for Chad, who had been through a tortuous few years before turning to teaching online. His real estate business imploded during the 2008-2009 recession, and his wife was actually deported due to immigration issues. He spent 5 years apart from his wife, Ana, and their two young children before being able to reunite under one roof.

Chad made sure to mention that building his teaching business wasn't exactly a cakewalk, either. "I believe my longest day was actually 16 hours," he said. "It was life or death. I had 3 people depending on me, and I couldn't let them down."

Today, the family lives in Central America where Chad works barefoot and doesn't stress about commuting or office politics.

On Verbling, you can set your own rates for online language lessons. Most teachers charge between $10 and $25 an hour, and you can hire Chad for $24-26 per hour—when he's not fully booked.

Other Platforms to Consider

Motaword – If you speak multiple languages, you can earn money translating text with Motaword.com.

SpeakWrite – Complete audio to text transcriptions for legal, government, and private sector clients. According to its site, the average SpeakWrite.com transcriptionist earns $300 a month, while top earners are bringing in $3,000+ a month.

Translate.com | Translatorsbase.com – Get paid by the word to translate text.

Unbabel – Earn $8-18 an hour translating one of 28 languages for customer service teams around the world on Unbabel.com.

italki – Set your own hourly rate for Skype language lessons and conversation practice sessions on this platform with more than 2,000,000 language-learning students. When I was browsing italki.com, it seemed like rates were mostly around $10 an hour for English practice.

VerbalPlanet – VerbalPlanet.com is another peer-to-peer language learning site where you can set your own hours and rates. The average student payment is $22 for a 45-minute lesson, and VerbalPlanet asks you to only apply to this tutoring platform if you have teaching experience.

Rype – The Rype app connects language tutors with language learners all around the world. Rype handles the scheduling and payments, and you focus on creating helpful lessons and conversations. Getting accepted may be a challenge, though; Rype claims its average teacher has more than 7 years of teaching experience and that it only hires the top 1% of applicants.

Myngle – Teach your native language to professional business travelers online through Myngle.com.

<u>Interlinguals</u> – Create a profile on Interlinguals.com and earn $15-50 an hour having conversations with language learners locally or online.

The Next Level: Building Your Own Brand

One person who's turned her language skills into a serious standalone business is Gabby Wallace. Gabby started out as a classroom English teacher in Japan, but now runs GoNaturalEnglish.com full time.

To fill time in between classes, she decided to start recording videos as extra learning material for her students.

Originally, she planned on emailing the videos to her students, but soon found out the files were too large. Instead, she uploaded them to YouTube and emailed the link to the videos instead.

And that's how, almost by accident, she took her local small group teaching to a worldwide audience. Over the next few months, the view count started climbing on YouTube and requests for one-on-one English tutoring and coaching started to come in.

The Power of Questions and Content Creation

Gabby continued to upload more videos while working full time in the classroom, often using questions from her students as ideas for her videos. She explained that she found most of her content ideas not from keyword research or SEO, but by "asking students what their problems were and what videos they wanted to see."

Indeed, content that answers specific questions is a popular way to help your audience and increase your odds of being discovered when someone else types a similar question into Google.

After doing one-on-one tutoring over Skype for around a year, viewers began asking Gabby if she had a digital course.

Since students were asking for it, she knew it was time to create a paid product.

Paid vs. Free Content

Since YouTube is a free channel, I was curious how Gabby had turned her educational videos into a viable business. Namely, if you're creating all this content for free, what will people pay for?

Gabby recommended offering different formats as a key distinction between free and paid material. The content may be similar, but the length and format are very different.

For instance, Gabby's YouTube videos are generally around 5 minutes long. They're long enough to cover the most essential points about a topic, while being short enough to keep her viewers interested and wanting more.

Her paid products, on the other hand, are much longer. Another interesting point Gabby made was that her YouTube content is 50% motivational and 50% practical. This is because staying motivated is incredibly important when learning a second language. In contrast, her paid products feature much more "how-to" and "follow along" types of content.

She uses YouTube as a free resource to attract an audience, and drives viewers back to her website with an offer for a free product in exchange for an email. Gabby explained that most of her course sales do not come directly from YouTube, but from the viewers who are engaged enough to join her email list. The sales come through after emailing them.

What Made Gabby Stand out in a Crowded Niche?

A lot of people thinking about getting started on YouTube are probably intimidated by the amount of other channels in their niche. Gabby thinks she stood out largely by being herself. Perhaps this is cliché, but your own personality is something unique that only you can offer. It's important to remember that if you start a YouTube channel.

I think Gabby's also been successful because she likes being in front of the camera. She's not afraid to be a bit "goofy," and she brings a fun, positive energy to her videos. She told me she's actually lost subscribers for not being super serious all the time, but many more people comment and send her emails saying they love her style.

It took Gabby 3 years for her channel to reach 10,000 subscribers, but in the 2 years since then, she's grown it to over 200,000 subscribers. She attributed the acceleration to paying more attention to how she named the videos. "Make sure your title includes your target keywords," she explained, "But also something unique about the video."

For example, she has a video called "Don't Be Shy! How to Start a Conversation with Anyone in English." I think that title is likely to appear in searches for keyword phrases like "how to start a conversation," "start a conversation in English," and "don't be shy." It's been viewed more than 750,000 times.

Monetizing through YouTube

Uploading videos to YouTube takes a lot of time and effort, but can serve as the foundation for a growing business, as it has for Gabby.

One way to monetize your channel is with Google's Advertising Partner program. Gabby has been doing this for several years, and it brings in $300-1,000 a month.

She mentioned she actually turned off the YouTube monetization for some of her most popular videos in order to promote her own products and email list sign-up instead. It cost her money in the short term, but has translated into more course sales and engagement in the long run.

Aside from her one-on-one tutoring and course sales, other forms of monetization she uses include working directly with sponsors, promoting relevant products and services as an affiliate, and participating in bundle sales with other online language teachers.

These bundle packages contain courses, videos, ebooks, and other products from all of the collaborators. By collaborating with other channel hosts, she can reach a much wider audience—a win-win for all the teachers involved in the bundle.

Sell Your Lawn Mowing Prowess

Love the smell of freshly cut grass? YourGreenPal.com connects homeowners with nearby landscapers and lawnmowers. Set up a profile, bid on the jobs you want, and get mowing.

Sell Your Legal Advice

UpCounsel.com is a growing legal marketplace that matches clients to lawyers with a specific area of expertise.

Attorneys can also use the LawTrades.com platform to connect with legal clients in a next-gen way.

Sell Your Mechanic Skills

YourMechanic.com gives certified auto technicians the chance to work flexible hours, earn $40-60 an hour, and choose which jobs to work on. The platform promises customers 30% savings over going to the repair shop or dealership.

The Next Level

Matt Bochnak runs a motorcycle repair business from his home in Chicago, Illinois (ChicagolandMotorcyleRepair.com). That on its own is a great side hustle, but Matt had the idea to begin filming himself doing the repairs. He now has over 19,000 subscribers on YouTube, and sells complete step-by-step do-it-yourself repair guides to other motorcycle owners through his website.

He said he now earns more selling the video guides than he does on actual repair work, and has been approached to create videos for Allstate's motorcycle insurance division.

Sell Your Music

Musicians can sell their music directly to indie music fans on Bandcamp.com, which has paid out more than $166 million to artists so far.

CDBaby.com calls itself the best independent music store on the web. In addition to its popular storefront,

CDBaby will help you sell your music in 95+ digital stores and 15,000+ brick-and-mortar locations.

Sell Your Photography Service

Professional photographers and videographers can use the SmartShoot.com platform to expand their client base and find new projects.

WonderfulMachine.com is a similar platform for photographers to connect with people who need their skills.

Sell Your Pictures

Another interesting angle for shutterbugs is the option to sell stock photography. These are the images that grace websites, brochures, and marketing material all over the world.

Dave Bredeson is a professional commercial photographer who supplements his commissioned work by selling stock photos on Dreamstime.com. Even though each image sells for relatively little, that same image can be sold to dozens of different buyers. In fact, Dave had around 3,000 images in his portfolio when we connected, but he'd made over 74,000 sales on Dreamstime.

"Lately I've been averaging around $1,600 a month in Dreamstime earnings," he explained. "I choose topics that are easy to produce at the lowest possible cost.

My portfolio is dominated by backgrounds, technology, business, and Christmas images."

Another Dreamstime photographer, Kevin Thomas, added, "You need to understand what types of images are in demand. Everyone should have a fair idea of what types of images have commercial potential because you are exposed to various types of advertising and marketing every day."

However, Kevin noted that the business is becoming more competitive. "I find myself working harder for less," he admitted, adding that he earns $7,000-8,000 a year on Dreamstime from a portfolio of 2500+ images.

"There is still great potential for selling images online," Kevin said. "It really boils down to how you manage your business and the level of quality you can produce." As the market has become more saturated both with amateur and professional photographers, it's forced photographers to step up their shooting and editing.

"The advantage of having a micro-stock business is you can put in as little or as much time as you desire," he added. "Being creative and artistic has its own personal rewards, and sometimes you will stumble into various types of niches where sales can be had."

Leez Snow runs EverythingMicrostock.com, a site dedicated to helping photographers earn money in this field. Leez, who sells on iStockPhoto.com, echoed Dave's sentiment that it's a volume game. "It's all about quantity," she said. "There's a mental leap photographers have to make to say, 'I will sell this image 100 times for $1 versus one time at a gallery for $100.'"

Stock photography started as a side hustle for Leez, but she now makes a full-time living selling her images. To improve your odds of making a sale, she suggested taking full advantage of the platform's keyword-tagging and image-naming tools. "Think of it like a Google search and all the ways people might search for your image."

Other Platforms to Consider

SnapWire – Earn 50-70% royalties when companies buy the rights to your beautiful photography on SnapWire.

Foap – Submit photos from your phone to Foap.com's unique stock photography website and earn $5 for every image you sell. I've thrown a handful of my pictures up there, but no takers yet.

PhotoDune – On PhotoDune.net, photographers can earn 55% royalties for their work or an even greater percentage for exclusively distributed images.

Pond5 – Pond5.com is a super cool site with not only photography, but also music, video, sound effects, and illustrations. As an artist, you can set your own price for your work and earn 50% royalties.

Clip Canvas – Sell video and film clips through the ClipCanvas.com search engine and directory.

Shutterstock | DepositPhotos | Fotolia | BigStockPhoto | Alamy – There are literally dozens of stock photo sites out there. If each platform doesn't require exclusivity, it probably makes sense to syndicate your work to all of them for the best chance of discovery and royalties.

Sell Your Skills (In-Person Freelancing Platforms)

Thumbtack.com is a freelance marketplace (in the US only, so far) that seems to be more oriented to local service providers. However, as freelance mechanical engineer Scott Tarcy found, it is open to remote work as well.

Buyers submit requests for what they need, and if it seems like a fit for your skills, you can bid on the job.

In contrast to other freelance platforms or bidding networks, only 5 people can bid for each job posted on Thumbtack. This means you're not competing with dozens of other applicants, which also makes the decision process faster and simpler for buyers.

On the downside, this means you need to be very quick to respond. Scott explained that having the app on his phone is the fastest way to hear about new postings. He gets push notifications when new jobs that meet his criteria are posted.

Thumbtack charges a flat fee of $7-12 per bid from you, the contractor. This compares to marketplaces like Upwork or Fiverr (see below) that can charge 5-20% of the value of the job, which can turn into some significant cash in a hurry. If you're doing a $500 job, it is *way* more attractive to spend $7 on a bid and win the contract than to pay $100 of your earnings as a platform fee. Once you win the job on Thumbtack, you keep 100% of the agreed-upon price.

Scott has kept a close eye on his ROI using the Thumbtack platform. When he first started out, he earned an average of $2 for every $1 he spent on bids. Today, he earns around $10 for each $1 he spends. Put another way, he spends $70 in bids to land $700 worth of work–all from clients he never would have heard of without Thumbtack. He added that you can claim a refund if you think you were part of a hoax bid, too.

Scott shared some of the best practices when bidding for jobs on Thumbtack:

- Have a standard email template so that you can quickly respond to jobs and be one of the first 5 bidders.
- Ask for more details when replying in order to start a dialogue with the client.
- Reply with a detailed and personal response once the client responds to you.
- If the client leaves a phone number, *call right away* and talk to the client directly.

The Thumbtack marketplace is pretty extensive, with services including accounting, house painting, voice lessons, quilting, web design, and even legal work. The company paid out over $1 billion last year.

Other Platforms to Consider

TaskRabbit – TaskRabbit.com is one of the largest sharing economy platforms, and you can create a profile specializing in everything from running local errands, assembling furniture, local admin temp help, and even virtual support jobs.

Rates vary widely based on what service you're providing, but I've seen tasks anywhere from $15 an hour all the way up to $100 an hour or more for specialized handyman skills.

Bonus: *Get $20 off your first task at sidehustlenation.com/taskrabbit.*

AskForTask – Sign up to do "task" work in your town like house cleaning, moving, or handyman projects on AskforTask.com, the leading task marketplace in Canada.

Airtasker – Airtasker.com is Australia's version of TaskRabbit.

Bark – Bark.com is a UK marketplace for service professionals. Join the network to get found and get jobs around your schedule.

Zaarly – Use Zaarly.com to get matched up with customers in need of home cleaning, yard care, and handyman services near you.

Handy – Earn up to $22 an hour as a cleaner or up to $45 as a handyperson. According to the Handy.com website, top professionals are taking home more than $1,000 a week. If you're skilled in painting, plumbing, electrical work, or cleaning with a friendly service attitude, this could be an interesting side hustle.

LocaWoka.ca – This Canadian firm aims to match busy homeowners with people like you to help them run errands, take care of laundry, and pick up items around town.

Sell Your Skills (Online Freelancing Platforms)

Fiverr

For me, Fiverr.com has been a fun and eye-opening side hustle experiment. Since I started on the site, I've earned over $11,000, met some awesome people, and experienced firsthand the power of marketplaces like the ones featured in this book.

On Fiverr, you come up with a base "gig"—something you can offer for an entry-level price of $5—and then add relevant upsells or packages to increase your order value. I've sold $1,000 projects through Fiverr, and one of my podcast guests claims to have sold the first $10,000 Fiverr project ever. So, even though the starting points are low, there's definitely money to be made.

You don't have to bid for jobs; in that sense it's a true Buy Button platform. You decide what to sell, and anyone who wants it can order it.

Initially, I was cautious to put anything up for sale that would require my direct time involvement to deliver. After all, working for $4 (after Fiverr's 20% cut) is not exactly a great way to get ahead in life.

So, I started out selling a couple of ebooks I had written and actually had strong results out of the gate. One title even surprisingly outsold Amazon.

As I got more comfortable with the platform, I decided to test out a new gig: mini 5-minute screen recording website audits.

The concept was simple. People would send me links to their websites, and I would give my opinion on ways they could improve them.

The videos took a few minutes to prep and ran 5-7 minutes in length, plus another couple minutes to upload and deliver.

If I was cruising through them back to back, I could generate an effective hourly rate of around $24 an hour. I ended up doing hundreds of these website audits over a year or so. Feedback from customers was good, it didn't take a ton of time, and it was actually pretty fun.

I was earning $200-400 per month with this little side hustle.

For my "gig extras," I offered a more in-depth analysis of a site's marketing or SEO options and a copy of my ebook, *The Small Business Website Checklist*. These gigs had an average order value of $14, well above the $5 minimum.

Not surprisingly, the majority of revenue came from a minority of the customers; 25% of the customers generated 70% of the income. Not quite 80/20, but close!

Nearly one-third of my customers ordered at least one "gig extra." I'm not sure what the Fiverr site-wide average is, but I felt like that was a pretty healthy percentage.

Later, I offered a non-fiction book proofreading and editing service through Fiverr at a rate of $5 per 500 words. Since most books are much longer than 500 words, this gig had a great average order value as well, and I got to read some really interesting—and some not-so-interesting—work.

Here's what I think makes for a successful gig on Fiverr.

1. Short Gig Title

Clear and concise gig titles perform better. It's difficult to fully convey the value of your gig in just a few words, so you should test out a couple different variations to see which one generates more interest or search volume.

Pro Tip: use the Google Keyword Planner to see which words tend to get searched more. Fiverr, like many of these other platforms, is a mini search engine.

Put yourself in your customer's shoes. What would they be searching for to find you?

2. Detailed Description

Buyers should know exactly what they're getting before they buy. This is your opportunity to sell your services and let customers know why they should do business with you.

If you're getting a lot of questions asking for clarification or details, your description probably isn't doing its job.

You can also use the description to promote and explain your gig extras in more detail.

Descriptions are limited to 1,200 characters, which really isn't very much, so you have to be concise. Fiverr does allow you some freedom in formatting with bold or italic font, bulleted or numbered lists, and text highlighting.

Take advantage of some of these features to enhance your description.

3. Video and Images

Fiverr reports that gigs with a video description sell 220% more than those without. Because of that, a video is pretty much a requirement.

My video isn't the highest quality material in the world; it's just me talking into my webcam. If you're not comfortable on camera, the funny thing is you can probably find someone on Fiverr to help make your gig intro video for you.

4. Targeted Upsells

The upsells, or gig extras, is where Fiverr gets interesting. The more orders you complete, the more opportunity you have to add higher cost upsells.

The trick I've found is to offer a few different options that might interest your gig customers.

You can change these extras and their pricing at any time, so there's no harm in testing different offers. Remember, the more you earn, the more Fiverr earns, meaning the company wants you to succeed and make sales.

5. Ask for Feedback

Fiverr's feedback system uses the familiar 5-star rating system.

Given that most people won't leave feedback unless prompted, I've added a P.S. script to each of my delivery templates that asks buyers to leave a "5-star rating" if they found the gig valuable.

With that in place, nearly 80% of my customers have left a positive rating. It's important to get some initial positive feedback on your gigs via friends, family, or customers who already love you.

6. Offer a Guarantee

I also make sure to include a 100% money-back guarantee on all my gigs. I feel like that helps persuade buyers who are on the fence about ordering.

The Next Level

In the case of my website audit gig, this would have been the perfect gateway introduction to a full-service web development agency. Quite often, I'd have Fiverr clients come back to me thanking me for the feedback on their site and asking if I could just make the changes I'd suggested.

Since that wasn't my focus and I didn't always have the technical chops to get it done, I'd have to decline. But if that was part of my business, I'm confident

Fiverr would have been a tremendous source of pre-qualified leads.

My Fiverr Transition: Selling Digital Products

Lately I've turned off my video site review gig and my proofreading gig, instead shifting back toward my original Fiverr strategy of selling digital products. These books and guides are great $5 offerings because they solve a specific customer problem, and you can create them once and sell them over and over again.

They don't bring in as much revenue as the freelancing gigs, but they don't take any time to deliver, either. And since the assets are already created, each sale is incremental profit.

You may find in browsing your hard drive (as I did) that you already have some useful guide you wrote or recorded that would be perfect to re-purpose to Fiverr.

For inspiration on what you can sell either as a service or a digital product, take a look at some of the top-sellers in each category. With those gigs, you know there's a proven demand. As the seller's time-to-deliver gets bumped further and further out due to increasing demand, it creates opportunity for you to come in and offer a similar service with a faster turn-around time.

Bonus Section: 5 Fiverr Gigs with High Average Order Values

Fiverr may have started as the $5 marketplace, but savvy sellers know there's potential for much higher earnings on the platform.

These opportunities come in the form of gig extras (upsells), multiple orders, packages, and the custom offer tool. With the custom offer tool, you can now actually make sales up to $10,000.

But if you're just starting out as a seller, it can be tough to identify which gigs have high average order values. For its part, Fiverr now encourages buyers to spend more than the base-level $5 by showcasing sellers' "packages," but you can also take matters into your own hands by highlighting your gig extras in your description and your gig promo video.

Here are a few examples of gigs you may be able to offer that tend to have higher average order values (AOVs).

1. Proofreading and Editing

Since most proofreading gigs are priced by the word, there's a natural opportunity to have high-priced orders. The base-level $5 gig will generally get you 500-1500 words worth of proofreading, but a full-length book may be 20,000 words or more.

At the $0.01 per word rate, that 20,000-word book is a $200 order.

I actually got many of my early non-fiction editing clients through Fiverr. One book ended up being over 100,000 words, and the author became my first 4-figure Fiverr client. (We broke up the job into several smaller sections.)

2. Voice-overs

Similarly, voice-over work is priced by the length of the recording. The base-level $5 gig will usually cover scripts between 50 and 100 words, but if you need more than that, you're into the gig extras.

Also in your upsells, you can offer different file formats, background music, or faster delivery. For example, I ordered my podcast intro from Fiverr, and it was $15 because it included an intro, outro, and background music.

As a seller, I did one voice-over gig (by request), and it was *way* harder than I imagined to read the script word for word with intonations that made sense. Haven't tried it again since!

Still, if you have the microphone and the recording software already, this could be a fun one to get started with.

3. Transcriptions

Although I had a hard time finding a good transcriptionist on Fiverr, I'm sure they're out there. Most of the base-level $5 gigs offer to transcribe between 5-20 minutes of audio. If you can attract customers who have an hour-long podcast, you're looking at $15 to $60 per order.

And since most podcast hosts produce a new show regularly, you're setting yourself up nicely for repeat customers.

For additional gig extras, you can add faster turnaround times or special formatting based on client requests.

4. Book Covers

Book covers and other graphics are a great opportunity for upsells and repeat business.

Even if the base $5 gig promises a fresh cover design, you can include extras for high-resolution graphics, multiple variations, different file formats, and front-and-back covers for hard-copy versions.

5. Copywriting

Just like with the examples listed above, you can find amazingly talented writers on Fiverr, but they probably won't be the ones offering 500-word articles for $5.

As a seller, there are some cool opportunities to work with high-value clients.

Writing gigs are typically priced based on the word count without much attention paid to the amount of research involved. If you can set a reasonable rate per word and attract repeat clients or customers looking for longer form content, you can get your average order up to $20 or more.

Especially if customers are looking for regular blog content with a consistent voice, you could become their go-to writer.

I believe the highest order values come when you can differentiate yourself further by specializing in a certain niche or type of copywriting. The right words for the right client can be worth a lot of money.

Your Turn

What Fiverr gigs could you offer? Hopefully, these examples got the gears turning and showed that Fiverr has a world of opportunity beyond just $5 gigs.

What I'd do to get started is take a look at some of the sales pages and videos from top sellers and try to emulate what they're doing, but add your own unique spin.

One thing to keep in mind with freelancing on Fiverr or any other platform: there will always be a cheaper offering, but you can't race to the bottom on price.

After you've built a little bit of a portfolio, stick to you guns and don't succumb to the pressure to lower your rate.

Upwork

Any discussion of online freelancing would be incomplete without mentioning Upwork. Upwork is the lovechild of Elance and oDesk, the two largest freelance marketplaces.

With Upwork, you create a profile and bid on jobs that meet your criteria. There's a bit of an art and science to it, and while you'll hear some complaints about cheap clients and stiff competition, I keep hearing success stories of people finding quality work.

For example, my friend Jesse Gernigin is a professional hypnotist who supplements his income with copywriting projects on Upwork. He attributes much of his success on the platform to "understanding human nature."

Even when competing with people who are smarter and more professional, Jesse said he wins freelancing gigs by having a better understanding of what clients want to hear and communicating how he can help them.

Specifically, Jesse uses Upwork to find clients who will offer him more work in the future after he's secured the first job. While it's not foolproof, he's found that clients often give off subtle signals that indicate the potential for recurring work.

For instance, you can see clients' spending history on the platform, their feedback ratings and comments, and whether or not they've posted similar jobs in the past.

An interesting point Jesse raised is that some proposals will say something along the lines of, "If we like you, we are going to keep hiring you." To him, this is actually an indication that the client will *not* re-hire someone, and is just a ploy to attract more competitive bids from freelancers.

Naturally, repeat business from customers you love working with makes life easier for everyone involved and can dramatically improve your effective hourly rate because you're not spending as much time writing proposals or bidding for new work.

The biggest challenge for starting on any new platform is making sales when you don't have any feedback ratings yet. One strategy is to offer your services at a discounted rate to attract those first few clients because they're essentially taking a risk on you that you're legit.

Indeed, I've heard that advice from several successful freelancers on the podcast before: undercut the competition by 15-20% to build a portfolio and earn some initial positive feedback.

While that strategy can definitely be effective, Jesse says it isn't always necessary. As long as your rate is fair, he advised not to give into the bargain-basement pressures. For instance, he started out at $65 an hour and recently increased his rate to $95 an hour.

If you want to command premium rates—or even competitive rates—you need to build up a relationship with the client first.

Jesse shared some of the tips he uses when putting together a proposal for a freelance job on Upwork:

- Don't spend time recording a personal video. I think this tactic could definitely make your proposal stand out, but Jesse explained you're better off spending a fraction of the time writing a great proposal. He says he can bang out a well-crafted proposal in 5-10 minutes.
- Use the client's first name. This makes the proposal more personable and increases the open rate.
- Rewrite part of the request back. This shows the client that you're not using a copy and paste template.
- Explain to the client what's needed, how you can deliver it, and what the result will be.
- Share your experience with similar jobs and what the results were to help the client understand what you can do.

Jesse also shared what he calls "the gratitude theory." This means showing clients that you're grateful to be working with them and you appreciate it. This makes clients more inclined to send more work your way as they know you appreciate working with them.

The Next Level

Jesse added that the more hours you work on the Upwork system, the more visible your profile becomes to prospective clients. This leads to more "private invites"—potential customers *asking* you specifically to submit a proposal for their job. In this way, success breeds success, giving you a leg up on the competition.

Other Platforms to Consider

Freelancer.com | PeoplePerHour | Twago | Guru | People as a Service – Guru.com was the first freelance site I used as a client way back in 2005. Freelancer isn't my favorite freelancing platform, but it still has plenty of buyers. PeoplePerHour is quite popular in the UK. All these sites and similar ones operate in a common way, connecting freelancers with clients and taking a cut of the job.

TopTal – If you're an expert developer and willing to put your skills to the test, you can earn great money working remotely for clients on the TopTal.com platform. It's serious about the "top talent" thing, though, only hiring the top 3% of applicants.

FreeeUp – Earn up to $50 an hour, depending on your skillset, on this new freelance platform that matches you with businesses that need your help. Two rounds of Skype interviews are required to maintain the high quality of service providers on the FreeeUp.com platform.

Konsus – Join the global team of Konsus.com freelancers and get paid to serve clients in your area of expertise on your own schedule. Konsus advertises a "steady stream" of work and no hunting for jobs.

Needto – Join the Needto.com marketplace for access to flexible local and virtual jobs in your area of expertise.

Growth Geeks – The unique GrowthGeeks.com freelancing platform is specifically built for recurring monthly engagements. You'll find gigs for Instagram, infographics, SEO, and more, ranging from $49 to $500 a month and beyond. Apply to become a certified Geek to get your service on the marketplace.

Topcoder – Topcoder.com has paid out over $80 million to its community of designers and developers, who compete in company-sponsored crowdsourcing contests for cash.

Torchlite – Torchlite.com is a new freelance platform, specializing in digital marketing. If you're a blogger, email marketer, or social media enthusiast, apply to join the network and connect with clients all over the country. One thing that sets Torchlite apart is its focus on 12-month contracts, so freelancers can establish a long-term working relationship with clients, follow campaigns through to completion, and earn a consistent monthly income.

Moonlighting – The GoMoonlighting.com platform was built specifically for side hustlers. Post your offer or your skills for free and connect with buyers locally and across the country.

> **Bonus:** Want to learn more about starting a freelance or consulting business? Download the free Freelancing and Consulting bonus at BuyButtonsBook.com/bonus.
>
> Inside you'll find examples of how to determine what service you can offer, how to proactively approach potential clients, and how to position yourself to command premium rates.

Sell Your Smarts

The Savvy.is online teaching marketplace focuses on music, business, and coaching in addition to academics. Singing instructor Molly Rosen has turned her Savvy profile into a full-time business, teaching voice lessons, music theory, and ear training both online and in person (when the students are local).

Molly said the platform allows her to teach people all over the country and even internationally, working with students from preschool age all the way to seniors. The secret to her success? "I try to make sure everyone who works with me *loves* singing!" she explained.

Molly charges $55 for a 50-minute lesson and has completed hundreds of lessons since joining the platform in 2015.

On Wyzant.com (pronounced like "wise ant"), academic tutors are free to set their own schedule and rates, and the rates actually seem pretty attractive. For example, when I searched for math tutors nearby, the Wyzant search engine suggested tutors from $40-60 an hour.

The site is a popular online and in-person tutoring platform, helping students in 300 different subjects and all grade levels.

Mike Marani, an assistant principal in the Boston area, said he connected with local tutoring clients on the site and earned $360 a month for a couple hours of work each week. "I tutored algebra and math SAT prep," he explained. "As far as my profile, I think what helped me was the geographical factor. It was a home tutoring service, so I was only competing with people within driving distance that taught my specific topics."

Mike added, "Because I was entering homes, I made sure my picture was professional and inviting."

Dan Khadem originally created a Wyzant profile in 2012. "I needed to earn some side income, so I added my areas of expertise: Microsoft Excel, Outlook, PowerPoint, and Access," he explained. "Nine out of 10 of my sessions are on the Microsoft Access database software; I got students pretty quick because there was so little competition on Access."

Dan is a database developer for a Denver-area hospital by day, and said he tutors 4-6 hours a month at $45-55 an hour. He echoed Mike's findings in that almost all clients end up being local, and the first session is always in person. After that, he found that about half of his students are open to virtual sessions, which obviously saves travel time and expense.

The interesting thing is that most of Dan's tutoring clients aren't really students; they're companies. Employees have been tasked with figuring out a database problem, and happen upon Dan's Wyzant profile while scouring the Internet for help. After hiring him for a "tutoring" session and seeing the immediate value, many clients have uncovered additional database struggles they could use help with. This has led to some lucrative database consulting work for his side business, MicrosoftAccessHelp.net, which Dan said will easily surpass $10,000 this year—far more than he'll earn directly from tutoring.

His tip for improving your visibility on the platform is to actively solicit reviews from your students. "After each session, I send a summary of the lesson," Dan explained, "And at the end of the summary, I add, 'If you're satisfied with your session, the best compliment for me is a positive review.'" That one line tremendously helped increase the number of reviews, which helped give prospective students the confidence they needed to click the Buy Button and book some tutoring time with Dan.

The biggest complaint about Wyzant is its aggressive commission structure. For your first 20 hours of tutoring, the company takes a 40% cut, which is noticeably higher than nearly every other marketplace I've researched for this book. As you work more hours, that rate gradually steps down to a minimum of 20%.

The Next Level

Mario DiBartolomeo has been a full-time math tutor for the past 8 years in the Detroit area. He started working part time one night a week at a local tutoring center, but soon struck out on his own and began landing his own clients.

Today he runs MariosMathTutoring.com and even has a book called *Make Tutoring Your Career* to help others break into this field.

Mario gave me these recommendations for people looking to start and grow a tutoring business:

1. Put the word out to friends, family, and colleagues through Facebook, etc.
2. Contact the local schools and get on their tutor list.
3. Put up an inexpensive website that shows up in local search.
4. "Flyer" local high-end neighborhoods and coffee shops.

5. Put a small ad in the local paper near the beginning of the school year.

"Once you get the whole thing rolling," Mario said, "Students and families stick with you and start referring others... and you can adjust your prices from there."

Other Platforms to Consider

Studypool – On this homework Q&A site, tutors earn money answering questions on their own schedule. Studypool calls itself "the Uber of education" and reports top earners making $75k a year and other dedicated tutors making $500 a week part time.

Chegg – Chegg.com runs a popular online tutoring platform where top tutors earn $20+ per hour and $1,000 a month part time.

Tutor.com – Tutor.com is one of the largest online tutoring marketplaces with millions of sessions booked through its system. Tutors earn a set hourly rate, depending on the subject they're approved to teach in.

TakeLessons – Teach your favorite subjects on TakeLessons.com (in person or online) and earn $20 to $65 an hour on your own schedule.

UniTuition – UniTuition.com is a peer-to-peer university tutoring platform in the UK.

Classgap – Classgap.com is an all-online tutoring platform with coverage in more than 90 countries.

Homework Market – Students post questions on HomeworkMarket.com, and you can submit answers in your area of expertise. Previews are visible, but students have to pay to see your full response. According to the site, top earners have made over $100,000 on the platform.

University Tutor – Set your own rate between $10 and $250 an hour on UniversityTutor.com, a tutoring marketplace specializing in in-person academic assistance.

Course Hero – Help millions of students study smarter by uploading your course notes. You get paid when your content results in a new student joining CourseHero.com, and you can also earn by answering student questions on the platform.

Nexus Notes – If you have college course notes "rotting on your hard drive," you can upload them to NexusNotes.com for the chance to earn money when current students buy them. The site sets the price at $35 and pays a 50% commission to you, the contributor.

Sell Your Voice

I think we can all agree that getting paid to talk is a pretty sweet gig. I mean, that's something almost everyone can do, right?

I sat down with professional voice actress Carrie Olsen, who turned her voice-over side hustle into a full-time career in just 4 months. She assured me there was more to it than just talking, and emphasized the *acting* part of the profession.

There are auditions you have to submit, industry knowledge you have to learn, and hours of practice you have to put in. But hey, I practice talking every day, so I was curious how she landed her first clients.

As a podcast host, Carrie already had the equipment needed to make a high quality audio audition. That also gave her a level of comfort and confidence behind the microphone that many new sellers might not have.

Still, no one had ever paid her for this type of work before. To kickstart her business, she decided to join Voices.com, the #1 Buy Button marketplace for voice-over talent. Voice actors and actresses can join at either free or premium levels ($50 per month or $400 per year) and can create their own profiles and audition for publicly posted jobs.

You don't need any formal qualifications; you can get started with just a microphone and your voice. The monthly subscription fee filters out some people, but like the other platforms we've seen, there is still a lot of competition.

Carrie's advice was to audition for as many jobs as you feel you're a fit for and not to get discouraged if your first 10 or 20 don't result in a paying contract. Eventually, one will hit.

For auditions, clients will typically provide a script or part of a script. You then record the voice-over and send a copy of the file to the clients. They listen to all of the submissions and contact the person they want to work with.

Carrie's first gig was for a company in Denmark that wanted some voice-over work for a short video it was submitting to a film festival. The job went well and marked the start of a new career.

How Much Does Voice-Over Work Pay?

On the voice-over marketplaces there will usually be a budget or a range for the job. You can bid within the range or with an amount you feel is fair. There is a large variety of voice-over jobs, ranging from quick 20-second reads to full-length audiobooks.

And the pay scale runs the gamut as well. For the trailer of a multimillion dollar blockbuster movie, the pay is exceptionally good. At the other end of the spectrum, you can book someone on Fiverr, as I did for the intro for *The Side Hustle Show* podcast.

Like most freelance work, if you're good at what you do, you will find better paying jobs and positive word-of-mouth referrals. Carrie started doing more auditions, and the work starting becoming more frequent.

Her third job was for REI, the outdoor clothing and equipment chain. For over a year, she was their voice on radio ads, cinema ads, Spotify ads, and more. This was the tipping point where she knew voice-over work could replace her day job.

As far as best paying jobs go, Carrie's top job was $3,000 for under an hour of work. While this isn't a typical rate, it's an illustration of how lucrative this industry can be when you've established yourself.

What are the Startup Costs?

Carrie already had her recording equipment from podcasting, but the startup costs are not high for good quality equipment.

Carrie recommended the AKG Perception 120 XLR Condenser Mic, which is around $95, and the PreSonus AudioBox, which is around $100. She pointed out that any microphone that plugs directly into a USB port probably isn't going to be high enough quality. Go through the XLR mixer and then into the USB to add that extra touch of quality.

Carrie also explained that she paid for some voice-over coaching lessons with Alyson Steel, a veteran of the industry. She found these lessons to be very valuable, covering a lot of the industry knowledge and terminology, as well as how to approach reading scripts for auditions.

The Next Level: Proactive Outreach

After using the Voices.com platform and some of the other marketplaces below to land her first gigs, Carrie is now focusing on building her own brand. She has created a dedicated website for her business at CarrieOlsenVO.com, which showcases some samples of her work and invites brands to get in touch.

Instead of sitting back and waiting for auditions to come across her desk, she now targets companies she wants to work for and proactively contacts them. She especially focused on the e-learning market, reasoning that there are a ton of corporate training and orientation videos that need someone to voice. This strategy opened the door to her working with Disneyworld, the University of Virginia, and AT&T.

Today, Carrie puts in about 20 hours of work a week into her voice-over business and loves that it allows her to express her creative side and get paid while working from home.

Other Platforms to Consider

Voice123 | TheVoiceRealm.com | Bodalgo.com | VoiceBunny – These are some additional popular marketplaces for voice-over talent.

ACX.com – The Audiobook Creation Exchange is an interesting Amazon-owned platform that connects authors with professional narrators to—like the name suggests—create audiobook versions of their books.

Narrators can accept projects on a flat-fee basis or do the work for free in exchange for a percentage of future royalties. That option seems compelling because if you can build up a library of different titles that sell well, you can essentially earn passive or residual income from work you did once.

Sell Your Wisdom

Clarity.fm is my favorite by-the-minute consulting platform, and I've earned over $3,000 lifetime through the site. You can set your own hourly rate, add your areas of expertise, and accept consulting calls in your spare time.

Clarity earnings are incremental. I say that because my "clients" don't have a pre-existing relationship with me, but this platform brought us together.

I'll share how the platform works, how to set up your expert profile for success, how to earn your first reviews, and my tips to maximize your earnings.

What is Clarity.fm?

Clarity is the marketplace to get one-on-one expert advice on a wide variety of business topics. The site makes it easy to facilitate quick, Q&A-style consulting calls, and they connect 12,000 of these calls every month.

You can even talk to "celebrity" entrepreneurs like Eric Ries and Mark Cuban. Cuban, the Mavericks owner and Shark Tank investor, has his rate set to $166.67 per minute, though, and doesn't appear to have fielded any calls yet!

Clarity is a great Buy Button marketplace. People are there looking for answers to specific questions—and even better, they're ready and willing to spend some money for help.

For service-based businesses and consultants, this is another way for clients to discover you—one that doesn't rely 100% on your own marketing efforts.

It's not passive income, but there's also very little overhead involved. Once the call is scheduled, you can dial in from anywhere. I've taken calls from an Airbnb apartment in Madrid, a Starbucks in Seattle, and while walking around the streets of Anaheim.

My average call lasts 15-20 minutes and earns $35-40.

How Clarity.fm Works

Clarity connects experts to people who need advice. Once you create your profile and add your areas of expertise, you'll give yourself the chance for callers to discover you in Clarity's search engine.

The company provides a conference call number to dial in to and tracks how long the call lasts. You earn money for every minute both you and the caller are on the line. The company takes a 15% cut on every completed call.

If you have a website or blog, you can link to your Clarity profile from your sidebar, your about page, or your email signature.

Setting Up Your Clarity Profile

The first thing you need to do is to create an expert account, which is free.

Next, Clarity offers a few ways to "verify" your account with other social media profiles, and at the very least you must connect your LinkedIn account. (It's required.)

While I can't be sure, I imagine these verifications are a "ranking factor" in Clarity's search algorithm. They are also a way to ensure that you really are who you say you are—so people like me can't pretend to be Mark Cuban and charge $167 a minute!

In any case, they make your profile look more legit because they're prominently displayed on your profile page.

Upload a professional picture—or one related to your industry—as long as it shows your face.

If you're feeling super ambitious, you can now even add a video to your profile page. (I haven't done this yet.)

Setting Your Rate

When setting up your profile, you'll be asked to set your hourly consulting rate. Rates on Clarity start at $60 per hour, but generally average $100-300 per hour.

You can start out charging nothing to build up a base portfolio, but if you set your rate to $0, you won't be eligible to appear in Clarity's search results. (More on taking free "portfolio-building" calls below.)

On your public-facing profile page, rates are displayed by the minute. This may be a psychology hack. Does $1.67 per minute sound more affordable than $100 per hour?

There are a couple pricing strategies to consider.

The first would be to price low initially to help build up a bit of a portfolio of positive feedback. This would also be the strategy to consider if you envision Clarity being a potential lead-generation platform for your larger business.

Think of this just like Costco giving away free samples. The store is willing to give you a taste for free in the hopes that you'll buy a whole pack.

Another pricing point to consider is if you have publicly listed your rates elsewhere, then it may not make sense to "undercut" yourself on Clarity. After all, if you're an attorney who bills $400 an hour, you don't want clients learning they could have hired you for $100 an hour on Clarity instead.

Still not sure what to charge? Take a look at what others are charging for your areas of expertise (see below) and pick something in the middle.

When I'm shopping for goods, I tend to gravitate not toward the cheapest or the most expensive option, but toward something in between. Callers on Clarity may behave similarly.

You can change your rate at any time. I started out at $60 an hour and have been slowly increasing my rates as I've accumulated more calls and feedback ratings.

After you've made some money, you can withdraw your earnings to PayPal, or you can elect to donate your Clarity earnings to a charity of your choice.

Your Areas of Expertise

Each expert on Clarity can have up to 5 areas of expertise. Naturally, it makes sense to fill out all 5 to give yourself the best shot of being discovered.

Like all marketplaces, there's a search engine element to Clarity. Think of your expertise headings as your main keywords, like you would SEO keywords for a blog or website.

You also have the ability to add a picture to illustrate each area of expertise and write a little description. I like to have fun with the images, but I think of the written description as an online resume.

If you have any concrete deliverables or results you can share, all the better. Remember that on a page of text, people's eyes are drawn to numbers. You could include figures like:

- How big a budget you manage.
- The financial results you've achieved for clients.
- The percentage growth you've seen year-over-year.
- The number of visitors to you website.
- How many years of experience you have.

Even a brief call to action like "schedule a 15-minute call today" can be effective.

Since people don't know you here, they need to know why they should trust you to help them.

Building Your Profile: Your First Calls and Reviews

Whenever you start on a new marketplace, you're starting from scratch, so it's on you to give your profile the initial push it needs to get some real attention.

Thankfully, Clarity is aware of this problem and has a cool workaround for new experts. (After all, the company wants you to succeed because that's how it gets paid.)

The best way to collect your initial Clarity reviews is to set up free calls through the platform. Each expert has the ability to generate a "promo" VIP link to share with friends, clients, or other trusted individuals. You'll find your VIP link on the Edit Profile screen of your account.

This may not even require a huge change in behavior. If you're *already* taking free intro calls with potential clients, why not just run them through Clarity instead for a couple months in order to build up your base?

The call count and reviews are social proof. They help build trust with your potential callers that you're legit and can help them.

Maximizing Your Clarity Earnings

On each call, you can get a feel for the type of customer you're dealing with. Some are happy with a long rambling conversation, while others have a precise pre-written list of questions they expect you to answer. Some, surprisingly, love to hear themselves talk and will dominate the conversation.

I'm an excellent listener when the clock is ticking!

Some Insider Tips:

It's generally easier to keep someone talking than to get a new client. Every minute on the call is more money in your pocket. Be helpful and honest, and speak quickly (you're the expert!), but also make sure to ask if there's anything else you can help with.

Sometimes a thoughtful (and hopefully insightful) probing question or two can uncover a new area of assistance the caller hadn't thought of. They'll be grateful you brought it up–or they'll politely decline.

After a brief intro, I like to openly acknowledge the dollars-for-minutes relationship:

"I know we're on the clock here, so if you're ready, let's get right into it. I understand you're looking for help with _____."

This is a subtle way of showing you understand and intend to be respectful of the caller's time and wallet.

The other thing I like to ask at the end of the call (especially when I know the answer) is: "Has this been helpful?" It's a little sales/psychology hack. You'll always get a "yes," and the more enthusiastic the "yes" is, the more permission you have to ask for a positive Clarity review.

"Has this been helpful?"

"Yes absolutely–thank you so much!"

"Great! After we hang up, you'll get an email from Clarity asking you to review our call. If you have a minute to drop in a 5-star/excellent rating, that would be a huge help and very much appreciated."

I also invite people to follow-up with me after the call:

"If you think of anything else, please feel free to shoot me a note on the Clarity platform or by email. Happy to help out as best I can!"

And finally, Clarity is a powerful networking platform. You'll learn about businesses and industries you might otherwise have never been exposed to. Make an effort to keep the relationships with your callers alive in the weeks and months following your conversation.

You never know who else you know who can help a caller or who else a caller knows who may be able to use your help. Plus, the person's already spent money with you, which makes for a good contact in my book.

Other Platforms to Consider

Coach.me – The coach.me platform boasts more than a million users, and you can set up an online coaching practice in the areas of leadership, health, business, habits, and more. Earn $100 an hour or more working one-on-one with clients.

PrestoExperts – Sign up to accept one-on-one consulting calls or live chats at a rate you choose.

This platform has more than 600 different categories to choose from, and some experts have thousands of reviews.

Noomii – Noomii (think "new me") is the web's largest directory of life and business coaches. The platform charges coaches a $397 annual fee, but offers a money-back guarantee if you don't earn at least that much business from connections made on the site.

SoHelpful.me – SoHelpful is an interesting platform where you can offer your assistance for free, with the theory that these free conversations can help bring in new leads.

Sell Your Writing

Amazon's Kindle marketplace is the largest peer-to-peer marketplace in the world for authors. You can publish your work and tap into a massive audience of buyers, especially if your book solves a problem in a unique way or you can market your way to the top of the charts.

Self-publishing is one of my favorite side hustles, and Amazon is another fantastic place to put your Buy Button and earn residual income from an asset you create once.

I remember the thrill I felt after receiving my first royalty payment from Amazon of $47.43 and thinking, "I did it! I'm a professional author!" Since then, I've earned thousands more in author royalties—nothing lifestyle-changing, mind you, but a pretty awesome way to both build authority in a niche and earn passive income along the way.

Lise Cartwright was a dissatisfied administrative assistant looking for more out of life, and she found it through writing. She's now the author of a growing catalog of books for "time-poor entrepreneurs" and new freelancers looking to move their businesses forward.

She quickly built an impressive portfolio of titles, including *No Gym Needed*, *Side Hustle Blueprint*, and the *Outsourced Freelancing Success* series. When we spoke, just 6 months into her career as an author, she was already earning $3,000-4,000 per month in author royalties.

Starting from Scratch

Although Lise had no formal writing experience, she began seeking freelance SEO writing work on oDesk and Elance (now combined and rebranded to Upwork.com, featured earlier).

Without any real plan, Lise accepted a lot of random jobs, from building mini WordPress sites to freelance writing gigs. She found herself saying "yes" to all the opportunities she could handle, and then turning to Google if the job required learning something new.

In the beginning, the projects she won on oDesk were really low paying (e.g., $5 for a 500-word article), but as she built her portfolio and gained more client feedback, she was able to command higher rates. One interesting hack Lise shared in finding higher paying jobs was to search by price first (for instance, $500 or $1,000) and then filter by category (e.g., "writing").

"Is This All There Is?"

As an illustration of the power of pre-existing marketplaces, after just 10 months of freelancing primarily on oDesk, Lise met her goal of replacing half of her current salary and was able to quit her day job.

She had several ongoing clients and was really motivated by the fact that she was in control of how much she earned. More jobs led to more income.

The downside was that she was still "trading time for dollars" and wanted to take things to the next level.

Freelance Writer to Kindle Author

When Lise first discovered self-publishing on Kindle, it was a foreign concept; she had never even downloaded an ebook before! As she studied the art and science behind creating a book and selling it on Amazon, she became convinced this was the natural next step in her business.

After all, freelance writing is great, but once that article is written and you get paid, that's the end of the story. With a book, you can sell that same work to hundreds or thousands of customers.

She told me she became "addicted to the writing process." Techniques like mind mapping made everything easier, and helped turn the daunting task of writing a book into smaller, more manageable actions.

Mind-mapping involves drawing a visual outline of your book on a large sheet of paper. You start in the middle with the core topic and then spider out to all of the sub-sections. For instance, with this book, I'd put Buy Buttons in the middle with lines connecting to Sharing Economy Platforms, Marketplaces to Sell Your Skills, and Marketplaces to Sell Physical Products.

From there, I'd add the next layer. For instance, I'd add Ridesharing Platforms and Home Sharing Platforms and connect those to Sharing Economy Platforms. Off Ridesharing Platforms, I'd connect Uber and Lyft. In this way, you can create a visual map of your entire book before you even write your first words.

Lise compared this strategy to writing mini blog posts, something she was very familiar with from her freelance writing work and found far less daunting than tackling a book project from a blank page with a blinking cursor.

The First Launch

Lise's first book was about something she'd personally been struggling with: finding the time to exercise. In *No Gym Needed – Quick & Simple*

Workouts for Gals On The Go, Lise focused on the workout-at-home corner of the women's fitness market.

Prior to the launch, she set up a landing page to collect email addresses of people who might be interested in the book, and offered a free copy to anyone who signed up before launch day. By teasing out the project on her social media channels, Lise built a "launch team" of about 30 people.

When the book was ready, she sent free copies to everyone who'd requested one, and asked them to leave an honest review on Amazon and share the book if they thought it worthy.

She promoted it through Facebook groups daily, shared it on social media, and submitted it to dozens of different free book-promotion sites. (These are sites that cater to readers looking for bargain books, and invite authors to submit their titles when they're free or on sale.)

No Gym Needed flew to the top of the charts in the Health and Fitness categories within 3 or 4 days of launching and ended up getting to #35 overall in the entire Amazon Free Store!

Here's a general breakdown of Lise's book launch pricing:

- Free for 3 ½ days – generated over 7,000 downloads.

- Switched to $0.99 and kept it there for the next week.
- Increased to $3.99. When we spoke 6 months after the launch, it was still selling 30 copies a day and was #1 in the Aerobics category.

Note: To price your book for free for a limited time like Lise did, you must join KDP Select, which gives Amazon exclusive distribution rights to your book for 90 days.

After her successful launch, Lise realized that this whole "self-publishing thing" could be scalable. She started thinking about building a catalog book business: a portfolio of titles that could provide enough income to support her lifestyle and to stop freelancing for good.

Building a Catalog

Her next project was to write the men's version of *No Gym Needed*, which she says hasn't been quite as popular as the original, but has still sold steadily.

In a burst of writing and publishing activity, she published 9 more books in a matter of a few months, including 2 titles in the *Side Hustle Blueprint* series and 7 titles in the *Outsourced Freelancing Success* series.

On top of that, she told me she has 30 more books already partially mapped out.

Keeping up the Momentum

To maintain healthy sales and high search rankings for all of her titles, Lise created a monthly to-do list for herself.

This entails checking all keywords and categories regularly. She makes any necessary changes, rotates keywords, and optimizes the books' descriptions to match. Since Amazon is a search engine for buyers, she's convinced those small tweaks really make a difference.

(In your Amazon author dashboard, you can assign up to 7 relevant keywords to help your visibility in Amazon's search results.)

She also continues to generate traffic for the books via her blog, Twitter, and Facebook, and regularly runs promotional events and special prices. She reported that her whole catalog of books enjoys a bump during these promotions, not just the titles on sale.

Lise pointed out that Amazon does a great job of promoting authors, sending marketing emails to customers with suggested titles. If you're performing well in a certain category and an Amazon customer has a history of buying books in that category, you're likely to be featured in a marketing email from Amazon. After all, the company makes money for each copy you sell.

(For books priced from $2.99-9.99, Amazon takes a 30% cut, and the author earns a 70% royalty.)

Paperback Editions

As an additional distribution channel, Lise recommended CreateSpace.com to sell print-on-demand paperback copies of your books. Since CreateSpace is owned by Amazon, the paperback listings show up right next to your Kindle edition on the Amazon site. Amazon prints and ships your books as orders come in, so you don't have to worry about holding and storing inventory.

I think having a physical copy of your book makes your listing appear more "official," and many readers still prefer to hold a hard copy in their hands. Indeed, Lise told me her CreateSpace earnings are around $500/month without any specific promotion.

Other Platforms to Consider

Smashwords – I use Smashwords to syndicate some of my books to the other marketplaces listed below, but readers can also buy books directly from the site. If you don't enroll in KDP Select, this is an easy way to get your work in front of more readers, though in my experience the sales volume is significantly lower than Amazon's.

iBooks – While Amazon commands at least two-thirds of the market share in the ebook industry, there are other players, including Apple's iBooks. I found the formatting requirements quite challenging to submit directly to iBooks, so I ended up using Smashwords' free syndication service instead.

Kobo – The Kobo eReader and Kobo apps have a decent user base, so it might make sense to publish your work here as well.

Nook – Barnes and Noble may be closing many of its brick-and-mortar stores, but the company has a loyal customer base that's embraced the online store and the Nook eReader platform.

Google Play – Just like Apple has iBooks, Google's app store has a section for books as well where you can potentially reach millions of Android users.

NoiseTrade – NoiseTrade is a unique site where you can upload your book and give it away for free in exchange for an email address from the reader. When I ran a paid promo with NoiseTrade, I added hundreds of new subscribers in just a few days.

The Next Level: Your Book as a Business Card

Many authors consider their book primarily to be an authority builder. It's been said that a book is the world's best business card, especially if you want to be seen as a leader in your field.

For example, Sean Sumner is a physical therapist in Sacramento, California. He's written two bestselling books on sciatica and neck pain, and now gets invited to speak at conferences and trains medical students, other therapists, and physicians. There's no question he's the go-to authority on the topic; after all, he wrote the book on it.

Others look at a book as a low cost entry point into their universe. For example, you can buy Tony Robbins' book for $10, or you can attend his $10,000 multi-day conference. You can spend $10 for Jeff Walker's *Launch* book, which (on top of providing a great deal of stand-alone value) introduces you to his $2,000 Product Launch Formula course.

And I should probably note here that while I don't have a $2,000 product to "upsell" you on, I expect this book will increase my perceived authority in the "side hustle" industry and introduce many new readers to my work at SideHustleNation.com.

Freelance Writing Sites

BoostMedia – If you have the gift for writing short, compelling ad copy for text advertisements, you can earn money on BoostMedia.com, a crowdsourced copywriting platform.

Copywriter Today – This subscription-based content creation site is often on the lookout for excellent part-time, US-based writers.

ClearVoice – ClearVoice.com is a platform to connect established online writers with brands and bloggers in need of high quality content. You can set your own rate and check out the writing opportunities that fit your areas of expertise and interest.

<u>Scripted</u> – Scripted.com is a high-end content marketplace where writers can set their own rates, and it features a system-wide price floor to make sure writers earn a fair wage.

<u>Contena</u> – Contena.co is an aggregator of paid writing opportunities, ranging from $0.04 per word all the way up to full-time positions.

<u>Copify</u> | <u>HireWriters</u> | <u>TextBroker</u> | <u>TheConte ntAuthority</u> | <u>iWriter</u> | <u>Zerys</u> – These are just a few of the content-writing services that aim to connect writers with people who need content. Often derided as "content mills," these sites don't offer amazing hourly rates, but you can work your way up the system and graduate to higher per-word rates and earn decent money, especially if you're a fast writer.

Selling Your Skills Wrap Up

As the economy shifts to more and more virtual work, selling your skills through online, on-demand marketplaces will only become more commonplace. In this section we looked at nearly 100 platforms to help you earn money with your unique talents, strengths, and skills.

Doing work you enjoy and are good at is a key ingredient to living a happy life, and these marketplaces allow you to do just that, often from the comfort of your own home.

We even examined a handful of marketplaces where you can package up your expertise into digital products to sell over and over again, like Udemy or Amazon's Kindle platform. Still, the most common gripe I hear about selling your skills is that it's often a time-for-money tradeoff.

If the idea of spending your free time toiling away for freelance clients doesn't intrigue you, I'd encourage you to focus on the more time-leveraged platforms. You may invest more time upfront without any payout, but ultimately the sales you make down the road won't require your direct input. Think how you can translate your skills from one-to-one to one-to-many, like Phil and Lise have.

In the next section, I'm going to expand on the idea of time-leveraged platforms, focusing on marketplaces to sell physical products. These platforms don't rely on finding freelance work or sharing assets you own. In some cases, you can create or source your inventory once and never have to touch it again.

Marketplaces to Sell Physical Products

"Once again, we come to the Holiday Season, a deeply religious time that each of us observes, in his own way, by going to the mall of his choice."

—Dave Barry

So far we've covered sharing assets you control and selling services you offer, skills you have, and digital products you've created. The next types of marketplace I want to discuss are those that help you sell physical products.

There are 3 primary "flavors" of the physical goods marketplaces I'll cover:

1. On-demand marketplaces
2. Homemade and handmade marketplaces
3. Reselling marketplaces

With on-demand marketplaces, you generally upload a file or design, and the company produces the physical item only when someone places an order. This keeps overhead low and allows you to test a variety of product ideas with very little risk. However, because items are usually created in individual batches instead of bulk orders, profit margins are lower.

Homemade and handmade marketplaces operate similarly, only you're in charge of producing and shipping the merchandise when the orders come in. The homemade and handmade markets capitalize on the "maker movement," a renewed interest in supporting small-business owners combined with a renaissance of small-scale manufacturing. You have flexibility over your products, pricing, and production, but will have to keep an eye on your own time input to make sure you're not toiling away for $3 an hour.

And finally, reselling marketplaces are where you can put your Buy Buttons for second-hand products, new items you acquired at a discount, and even items you've had manufactured to sell under your brand and labeling. These include household names like Amazon and eBay and represent a huge audience of buyers you can get in front of quickly. The downside is that they generally require some upfront capital to acquire your inventory, though I've seen people start with whatever they can afford and continue to reinvest their profits.

On-Demand Marketplaces

Kat Parrella was working full time for a big IT company in New York, but always had a creative side. "I have a background in art," she explained. "I paint and draw, and would do the occasional business logo or business card design if someone asked."

But these one-off projects were few and far between and not particularly artistic. It was hard to imagine earning enough from her design work to free herself from the corporate world.

When Kat stumbled upon Zazzle in 2010, she immediately saw the potential. The company provided a unique print-on-demand marketplace that connected artists and designers with customers looking for one-of-a-kind products. Today, you can find everything from posters and prints, to baby blankets and burp cloths, to shower curtains and dog collars.

Kat began creating stationery designs for Zazzle. "I'm the big party planner in my family," she said, "so wedding invitations, bridal shower invitations, and baby announcements were all a natural fit."

Artists on Zazzle.com set their own royalties. Kat told me that she charges 10% for most products and that the sweet spot for sellers on the site is generally 5-15%. That means that on a $2.00 wedding invitation, she'll earn $0.20. But if there are 100 guests, that multiplies to $20. Perhaps the more exciting aspect is that invitation is an asset Kat can sell over and over again. "I'm not just selling it to one bride," she explained.

She described the two major advantages of Zazzle as discoverability and logistics. "If you Google 'wedding shower invitations,' Zazzle is on the first page," Kat said. "That's a customer who never would have found me otherwise."

On the logistics side, the company handles all order processing, printing, shipping, and customer service. "I try and create new designs each week; you have to stay fresh," she said, adding that she wouldn't have time for the creative work if Zazzle wasn't handling all the customer interaction and order fulfillment.

Kat now runs her design business full time and said that Zazzle probably accounts for 60-65% of her revenue. "I never would have been able to do what I'm doing now if it wasn't for Zazzle," she explained, but added it took a long time to ramp up to that point. She told me that for the first couple of years it was a slow process of adding products and doing the design work late at night after her day job.

Still, it was a creative outlet and something she enjoyed doing. "To me, it wasn't work," she said, noting that she was earning a few hundred dollars a month within her first 6 months on Zazzle. "It wasn't much compared to the time I was putting in," she explained, "but it was play money to go do fun stuff with my kids, and I knew it could grow. Today, Zazzle is helping me pay for my kids' college education."

I asked Kat what advice she had for new sellers starting out on the platform, and she said first to create designs that are unique or special or that resonate with people for some reason. She emphasized that Zazzle is its own mini search engine and that it's really important to fill in your product pages with the appropriate description text and tags.

You can check out some of Kat's beautiful work at zazzle.com/kat_parrella and merrilypaper.com.

Other Platforms to Consider

Cafepress – Cafepress.com is one of the original print-on-demand stores, where you can submit your designs to be printed on shirts, mugs, hats, pillows, underwear, and more. Artists earn a royalty on every item that sells.

Spreadshirt – Spreadshirt is a popular print-on-demand t-shirt (and other merchandise) seller. How it works is you upload your designs and create your own storefront. When someone buys, you earn a royalty on the sale, but never have to touch the inventory or ship the product. The company does it all for you.

I actually tried to upload some "hustle"-related designs to a Spreadshirt shop last year, but never made any sales. I found the interface really clunky and confusing, but maybe I should give Cafepress or

Zazzle a try. (In fact, it probably makes sense to syndicate far and wide since the hardest part was coming up with the designs.)

I think this has the potential to be a really cool passive income stream, especially if your designs can begin ranking on their own in Google.

Society6 – Society6.com is a popular marketplace to find affordable products featuring the work of independent artists. You can set your own price on art prints and earn $2-10 per sale on t-shirts, phone covers, mugs, shower curtains, and more.

Minted – The Minted.com specialty store offers wedding invitations, stationery, home decor, and other items from independent artists and photographers like you. Earn cash prizes for one-off contests and commissions on ongoing sales of your work.

Redbubble – Join the network of more than 350,000 independent artists selling their creative work on Redbubble.com. You have 100% control over the price for your work, and most artists earn 10-30% of the retail price as their take home profit.

Teespring – With Teespring.com, you create your own unique t-shirt designs and then market them to relevant audiences, earning the spread between your purchase price and the cost to produce. The interesting thing about Teespring is unless your campaign hits a minimum critical mass of orders (that you set), nothing gets printed and nobody gets charged.

TeeChip – Teechip.com operates similarly to Teespring, but with slightly lower product costs.

Viralstyle – Viralstyle.com also works like Teespring in that you can create or upload your own custom t-shirt designs, set your own pricing, and make money on every shirt you sell. It also lets you open up your own Viralstyle storefront where you can group similarly themed designs.

Threadless – Create your own store and submit your t-shirt designs to Threadless.com, a fun community of independent artists and fans. Like other print-on-demand clothing sites, you make the spread between the purchase price and the cost, usually around $10 a shirt.

Threadless says it paid out $1.5 million to contributing artists in 2015!

Homemade and Handmade Marketplaces

With 25 million buyers and 1.6 million sellers, Etsy.com is the largest peer-to-peer marketplace for handcrafted items. You'll find thoughtful pieces for your home, office, kids, closet, and more. You can even sell digital items like planners and calendar templates.

Kara Lamerato is a former private banker who turned to Etsy when she wanted to earn a little extra money on the side after her wedding. Since guests had complimented her wedding décor and because she'd used Etsy as a buyer before, she decided to set up shop selling wine-themed wedding placecard holders.

Kara—now a work-from-home mother of two—has sold more than 2,500 orders through the Etsy marketplace.

Starting on Etsy

"I had very limited technical background or skill," she explained. "Etsy makes it very easy to set up shop."

It took about 2 weeks before her Etsy store, Kara's Vineyard Wedding, saw its first sale, a $70 order for a set of wine cork placecard holders. "It was the biggest rush!" Kara exclaimed, and more orders soon followed. "It got really addictive really fast."

Weddings turned out to be a great market because people tend to buy items based on the number of guests. An item might only cost $2 or $3, but multiplied times 100 guests, all of a sudden it becomes a sizeable order.

Kara explained that Etsy is like its own mini search engine, and is really popular among the brides-to-be she is trying to reach. To optimize her Etsy store, she focuses on keyword tagging and product names that include descriptive phrases like "winery wedding," "vineyard wedding," "wedding placecard holders," "wine cork wedding décor," and others.

The other thing she said helps her listings stand out is beautiful product photography. Since photography was a hobby of hers, she already had the camera and the editing software, and in a visual marketplace like Etsy, you absolutely have to have awesome pictures.

Each product you add costs a nominal listing fee of $0.20, and when products sell, Etsy collects roughly 6% for facilitating the transaction and for credit card processing. Kara explained it is a really small price to pay for all the infrastructure, marketing, payment processing, and support the company provides.

Another advantage of Etsy is you have very little inventory risk. "Someone buys it, and then I make it," Kara said.

Growing the Store

Today, Kara has more than 100 different products listed on Etsy, and each one gives her a new chance to be discovered by a buyer and to turn up in search results.

In addition to placecard holders, she's expanded her product line to include wedding favors, wine bottle stoppers, wine glass tags, and even keepsake Christmas ornaments. Many of the product variations and new additions have actually come from customer suggestions and requests. "Some of the products that are really popular—and that I still sell today—actually originated from a customer request," she explained.

Making the Products

"Almost everything I do is made to order," Kara told me. It's a labor-intensive process to physically hand-make the items; nothing is mass-produced. On the one hand, that care and uniqueness help make Kara's business and others like it a success, but on the other hand, it takes real physical work to produce each order.

I asked if that aspect of the business ever wore on her, and she was quick to set me straight: "It never gets old!" she explained.

She said her main production time is in the afternoon after her husband gets home from his teaching job and can watch the kids, but sometimes goes late into the evening. "I do what it takes," she said, adding that the work is still really fun for her. "I feel so fortunate to have this opportunity to run my own business, make this viable of an income doing it, and to be my own boss."

For new sellers on the Etsy platform, Kara recommended taking advantage of the company's resources, such as the blog and help center. "Etsy's success hinges on your success," she explained. "Etsy wants to make it as easy as possible for you to succeed."

The Next Level: Your Own Storefront

While Etsy still accounts for 75% of her sales, it's an established channel for Kara. So, now she is turning her sights to her presence outside the platform. "Marketing wise, traffic wise, Etsy is pretty much on autopilot now," Kara said. "All of my marketing efforts go toward my own store at KarasVineyardWedding.com."

There are a couple advantages of building up your own online presence outside of Etsy, including avoiding its sales fees and diversifying income streams.

Kara also mentioned she'd like to create an ebook to help brides with wedding planning and hopes to eventually build a real-life wedding venue. Both items can be a little more time-leveraged and don't require her to build and ship products each time an order comes in.

I asked if she'd considered hiring help on the production side, but she said she didn't really want the burden and headache of managing staff. When she reaches her own production capacity, she expects to either raise prices a little or to continue to look for more "passive income" growth channels.

One of her off-Etsy initiatives is *The Wedding Planning Podcast*, a twice-weekly audio blog that she hosts for brides-to-be. The aim of the podcast is to establish and grow Kara's own platform and brand awareness outside of Etsy, and it introduces brides to her products as well. She essentially "sponsors" her own show and credits the podcast for some of her strong business growth this year.

"I know weddings inside and out," she said, adding that an accessible audio blog is a unique way to reach brides without the visual demands a blog on the same topic would carry.

If you've got an artistic or crafty side, perhaps you can tap into Etsy's wide audience of buyers like Kara has.

Other Platforms to Consider

Storenvy – Sell your own unique clothing designs, jewelry, crafts, art and more at this growing peer-to-peer platform for indie artists.

It's free to open your own Storenvy.com shop, where you can upload your items, set your own prices, and get discovered by buyers on the platform. Storenvy takes a 10% cut on whatever you sell.

Zibbet – The Zibbet.com marketplace features the work of more than 50,000 independent creatives in categories like home, jewelry, handmade, and kids. Create your own online storefront for $4 a month, and there's even a tool that lets you syndicate your Etsy listings.

ArtFire – Artfire.com is a marketplace to sell handmade crafts, supplies, vintage goods, and art.

Folksy – Sell your "modern British crafts" on the UK-centered Folksy.com marketplace.

iCraft – iCraftGifts.com is another outlet to sell your handmade items "without borders."

Reselling Marketplaces

The business model of resellers is as old as business itself: buy low, sell high. It's the same model used by every store on the planet—either brick-and-mortar or online—and it's one you can use as well by tapping into some established marketplaces.

eBay

The granddaddy of all peer-to-peer markets has to be eBay, and this book would be glaringly lacking if I skipped over it. The venerable auction site was founded in 1995, is still one of the 10 most popular sites in the country, and helps move $80 billion worth of merchandise each year.

My own experience with eBay has been limited to selling unwanted items around the house, but thousands of people are using the platform as a sales engine for their businesses. One of those people is Darrel Fitzpatrick, who actually works full time as a sales rep in Atlanta, Georgia. When we spoke, he was excited because his account had just hit $100,000 in sales for the past 12 months.

Getting Started on eBay

Darrel started on eBay the same way most people do—by selling items that were collecting dust around his house. However, after selling almost everything he could part with around his home, he realized that profit came from having a consistent volume of items sold, not the odd hidden treasure.

Finding Inventory to Resell for a Profit

When Darrel was between jobs, he began trawling though Craigslist ads for up to 8-9 hours a day, looking for bargains that he could resell for a profit. He told me he would sometimes make 300 phone calls a day during this time.

This not only brought in a lot of inventory for Darrel to resell, but it also built up a large web of connections throughout the Atlanta area. He explained that at first he didn't really discriminate on what kind of products he was looking for, but soon found that used electronics like cell phones and laptops were both profitable and in steady supply.

Before long, Darrel had contacts in electronics stores and warehouses, who presented him with opportunities to bid on large pallets of electronic goods and to take advantage of store discounts.

Another eBay reseller I spoke to had a similar strategy for sourcing inventory. Rob Stephenson calls himself the Flea Market Flipper, and while it might not be the most glamourous side business, he earned $30,000 from it last year, working 10-15 hours a week. He blogs about his adventures at FleaMarketFlipper.com.

Rob's a real estate inspector by day, but you can find him at the Orlando, Florida, flea market every weekend, hunting for the next profitable "flip."

To source his inventory, Rob has a few favorite spots in addition to the local weekend flea market. Among them are classifieds sites and apps like Craigslist, OfferUp, and LetGo. He's also a regular at his local thrift stores, which help supply a steady stream of products to resell.

While Craigslist is very competitive because of its popularity, Rob explained there can still be some great finds if you act quickly.

So what does he look for?

"I look for odd items," he said. "I look for weird stuff."

Rob once bought a prosthetic leg for $30. He sold it on eBay the next day for $1,000.

One man's trash is another man's treasure, right?

Rob said most of his deals are sourced within 10 miles of home, but he occasionally will drive up to 2 hours for a profitable item he finds online.

He suggested searching Google for regular or seasonal markets in your area, as well as the newer online marketplaces.

On OfferUp, he found a high-end exercise bike used in physical therapy offices.

He discovered that in new condition these bikes often sold for $6,000 to $7,000, and he offered $200 for it—slightly less than what the seller was asking. The seller agreed, and Rob went on to resell it for $2,800.

Finds like these are rare, but paint the picture of what's possible if you're constantly on the lookout for potential deals. Rob explained, "The more unique or specialized an item is, the greater the profit potential."

Aside from looking for "odd" items, Rob told me he just tries to find as much information about a product as he can. Since there usually aren't any barcodes to scan, that generally means using his smartphone to check a brand name and model number, if applicable.

You can try asking the seller for some background on the item, but often they won't know any more than you, especially at flea markets. "They're probably reselling the item too—from a storage auction or estate sale or something like that," Rob explained.

If it seems like this business relies on taking advantage of people or ripping them off, he added, the sellers are also probably selling the item for a profit, and wouldn't agree to a deal if it wasn't in their best interest.

Armed with whatever information he can glean from the seller and from the item itself, Rob does some basic research on the free eBay app to see similar items' selling prices.

I asked Rob if he had any criteria when it came to expected profit margin or initial investment. "I generally won't buy anything I can't sell for more than $100," he explained. "A typical purchase is anywhere from $10 to $40. My wife is starting in this business selling baby items, and she won't buy anything for more than $3."

The eBay Learning Curve

Darrel admitted that at first he lost money on a few deals because he didn't understand the market, but he quickly developed some buying criteria and streamlined his eBay listing process.

Following this approach, he used the eBay completed listings search tool to estimate a likely final sales price for each item. The default search only shows current auctions and "buy it now" listings, which often go unsold because of overly optimistic seller pricing.

Armed with the completed listings valuation estimate, he aimed for 20-50% profit margins on each purchase, settling for lower margins on bulk purchases. That meant if he bought a phone for $200, he'd want to resell it for $260-300.

(It's important to keep in mind that eBay takes 10% of your final sales price as its fee for facilitating the transaction.)

Once he mastered this process, he began to narrow his focus to recently released items because they hold their value longer. Electronics age quickly since each new model that comes out decreases the value of older models instantly. There's also greater demand for gently used, newer technology and a more accurate and established fair sales price.

If the market is really that efficient, I was curious how Darrel was acquiring his inventory on the cheap. He explained that there are always people willing to sell because they need money fast.

I think Darrel's willingness to jump on the phone and talk to strangers certainly helped, as did the hustle he put into building his "supplier" network. In his words, "Good business is knowing people and how to talk to people."

He also suggested testing devices to make sure they are in sellable condition, meaning they aren't being financed and that they are eligible to activate on a new account.

When it comes to fixing broken items, Rob said, "I am always looking for items that don't need any repair, but the majority of rehab work I do myself. I utilize the power of YouTube to figure out how to fix some things."

He said the tools he uses most often are a multimeter to test electronics, a tape measure for dimensions, and the Magic Eraser for cleaning up marks.

Interestingly, the same things that drew Darrel to the popular technology niche are what shied Rob away.

"The market for used iPhones is pretty well-established and efficient—all sales will gravitate toward the average price," he explained. "With odd items, there are more inefficiencies and profit opportunities."

How to Sell on eBay Like a Pro

In addition to using the completed listing information to get an estimated value, you can also use that data to see how strong the demand is for a given item. Is eBay hosting dozens of completed sales for similar items each week? Or is the sales volume a little slower? Darrel explained that this is important because you want to be able to turn your inventory over quickly so that you can get your money back and reinvest the profits.

He begins his listings Saturday evening on the East Coast and sets them up as 5-day auctions. He said this is long enough to give the market time to respond and short enough to encourage buyers to bid.

While eBay allows you pay extra to spice up your listing with subtitles and bold fonts, Darrel said "by far" his best marketing hack is to start auctions at $0.99 and let buyers bid up the price to a fair value (and sometimes beyond). As the auction draws to a close, the competitive spirit among buyers comes out, and they may continue to outbid each other to secure the item.

Rob also uses Craigslist, OfferUp, and LetGo to sell his inventory, but said selling on eBay is his favorite. "With eBay, you can reach a nationwide or worldwide audience of buyers," he explained.

When crafting his listings, he sets the price at or around the projected value of the item he found during his research. In contrast to Darrel, he avoids auction listings in favor of "buy it now" listings instead.

"If I can get 7-10 people watching the item on eBay, I know I have it priced right, and it will usually sell," Rob told me.

If the item hasn't sold after 30 days, he lowers the price and repeats the process. The goal is to quickly sell items, but he admitted sometimes they sit in his garage and collect dust for months.

"I would just rather keep the item until it sells for what I am looking for," he explained. "This year I sold a Gagglia Cappucino machine that I had sitting in our guest room closet for over a year, but it made me $1,000 after I dusted it off."

If you're brand new to eBay, Darrel suggested using the marketplace as a buyer first to learn how it works and also to generate some positive feedback on your account. All eBay feedback is lumped into one number visible on your item sales page, and is an important signal to buyers that you're a trustworthy seller.

Carrying Out Fulfillment

Aside from sourcing inventory, my biggest pain point for the few items I've sold on eBay is dealing with the packaging and shipping. Naturally, Darrel had this down to a science.

Since he begins his 5-day auctions on Saturday evening, they end on Thursday evening. That gives buyers Thursday night and all day Friday to pay up. Then on Saturday when he's off work, he heads to the post office or UPS store and ships everything out.

Darrel and Rob's Advice for Beginners

For people just starting out, Darrel recommended spending some time on Craigslist to begin looking for items to resell just like he did. "Start finding those bargains, find a niche of products you're interested in, create a budget, and start scaling up," he advised.

Rob's advice for people getting started in this business was to be consistent and invest the time each week into product sourcing.

"If you're not out there finding deals, you're not making money," he said.

One of my biggest takeaways from chatting with both Darrel and Rob was the advantage of selling bigger ticket items. It's easier to make $50 on one deal than to make $1 on 50 deals.

Craigslist

Craigslist.org is the most popular classifieds marketplace in the US, and as one of the most heavily trafficked sites in the country, it represents a powerful Buy Button opportunity for resellers. And while our eBay sellers above mentioned Craigslist as a place to source inventory, it can be a place to resell it as well.

One person who's been doing that successfully for years is Ryan Finlay, who originally turned to Craigslist flipping to pull himself out of $25,000 in debt. Ryan makes a full-time living (and supports his family of 7) buying and selling items on Craigslist.

How it Works

Ryan's business revolves around finding "undervalued" items on Craigslist and reselling them. Much like Darrel found it easier to sell on eBay once he established a focus, Ryan concentrates on appliances.

It's the same "buy low, sell high" business model, where you get to keep the spread between your acquisition cost and the final sales price. And the beautiful thing is that nearly every city in the US (and many other places around the world) has an active Craigslist community where peer-to-peer commerce is thriving.

One advantage of Craigslist over eBay is there are no listing fees or seller fees; it's a free platform to use.

There are no technical skills required and very limited start-up costs. (Ryan started with just $200 in the bank.)

Drawbacks to Craigslist include a user interface that's outdated (to put it kindly), and each transaction has to be completed in person. That brings up safety concerns and can become time-consuming if you're trekking across town to meet with buyers or sellers.

Getting Started

Ryan was working as a contractor but wasn't in love with his job, so he began experimenting with Craigslist arbitrage on the side.

After a few initial "wins," including earning $250 on a refrigerator and $100 on a washer and dryer set, he decided there might really be an opportunity there.

He met with some friends at a coffee shop and told them his plans. They served as accountability partners, checking in with Ryan daily via email for the next 6 months.

Finding Undervalued Items

Ryan explained the key to this business is knowing what items are worth. That means you might spend a few days on your local Craigslist site, Amazon, or eBay to get a feel for what certain items might go for.

Ryan recommended starting with what you know so that your learning curve will be shorter and your response time faster. That way, when you spot something that seems like it might have some margin in it, you can act quickly.

For example, Ryan initially dealt a lot in home theater items because it was an area he was familiar with. He added that name-brand merchandise is important since many buyers will search by brand name, and those can command higher prices.

He also dabbled in furniture, bikes, electronics, and power tools before focusing on appliances. He runs the business out of his home and garage with no extra storage facility required, but he admitted that your capacity to move and store bulky items will limit which product categories you can buy.

Interacting with Sellers

If an item is very attractively priced, Ryan explained, "It is best to get on the phone and call the seller rather than respond by email." For other items, you can easily type out a quick email along with your offer price to see if there are any takers.

One thing that surprised me was that Ryan is not a ruthless negotiator when he shows up to pick up an item. Since this is his full-time business, every dollar he can knock off the price is an extra dollar to his bottom line. He explained, though, that the constant haggling can really wear on you and that there's no need to beat sellers up for a few extra bucks.

Logistics

If you have no means of transportation, you'll be limited to what you can carry in a backpack or on a bike. Ryan says he's seen little trailers hooked up behind Honda Civics and even bikes, but that a small SUV can fit most appliances. (A truck is only required for the largest items.)

I was curious what buyers think when they show up to Ryan's garage and see that it is filled with a dozen or more appliances. He said even though it's pretty obvious to buyers he's "in the business," no one yet has backed out of a deal because of it.

Have a Goal in Mind

Ryan determined he could support himself and his family if he earned just $100 a day from this business. That daily target gave him something tangible and attainable to shoot for.

Your number may be higher or lower, but I believe it gamifies the hustle a bit. Can you find $100 worth of profit today?

Making the Most of the Free Section

One of the greatest parts of Craigslist is the "free" section. In fact, whenever I post something for free, it's spoken for almost immediately. We've unloaded moving boxes, a dresser, and a desk that way.

I always thought the free section was an amazing opportunity because you could conceivably acquire your inventory for $0, which puts you in an incredible negotiating position when you go to sell—not to mention the enviable profit margins.

But because competition is so stiff for the free items—with people literally sitting on the page and hitting "refresh" in their browsers—you have to act quickly. I asked Ryan if he was ever able to score free inventory.

"Yes and no," he said. "If a really valuable item is offered for free, shoot the seller a quick note offering to *buy* it—and include your offer price in the subject line of the email."

He explained that gesture will often put you ahead of the masses of free emailers. After I shared this tactic with a friend, he sent me a note saying he'd used it to score a piece of furniture that ultimately made him $300.

Other Platforms to Consider

<u>Gumtree</u> – Gumtree.com is the most popular classifieds site in the UK and Australia.

<u>Kijiji</u> – Kijiji.ca is the leading Craigslist alternative in Canada.

<u>OfferUp</u> – OfferUp is a fast-growing marketplace to buy and sell goods locally. I've found its free, picture-heavy app addicting to scroll through and see what's for sale.

<u>LetGo</u> – The free LetGo app also has a growing audience of buyers and sellers for used local items.

Bonus Section: Using Craigslist to Launch a Service Business

Because so many people use Craigslist every day, it's also a surprisingly effective platform on which to launch a service business. When my wife was starting her photography business, she and her partner put an ad on Craigslist.

At the time, I thought that was a stupid idea— nobody's looking for wedding photographers on Craigslist! But I was dead wrong.

Within the first couple of days, they were flooded with inquiries and had more than enough work to fill their schedule and build out their portfolio.

A *Side Hustle Nation* reader pointed out there's even a section of the Craigslist site specifically for "gigs." So not only can you post your own services for sale, you can also see what opportunities are out there in categories like Computer, Event, Creative, Domestic, and Writing.

In 2015, Cassandre Poblah earned $2,230 in two months of side hustling on Craigslist.

Cass works full time as an administrator for a non-profit community center in Montreal, and her story illustrates the power of the marketplace.

Cass is the first to admit that $2,230 isn't a remarkable amount of money, but she said, "It helped me pay down a significant amount of my student debt in a very short amount of time, starting with zero money invested and zero experience."

"I had tried launching businesses in the past," she explained. "I would take months preparing the perfect plan, building and testing prototypes, and doing surveys and market research, only to get discouraged and quit after investing so much time into projects."

This time, she gave herself a one-day time limit. "I was sick of failing to launch. My sister and I talked about my idea for an hour. We wrote an ad in 15 minutes, and that very night I got two inquiries."

The next day, Cass had secured two clients. With no investment, no equipment, and no experience, in 24 hours she'd already done what her other business ideas never had—made a sale.

She credits the simplicity of her first step: "The decision I made was to just get started. It was to stop being scared, to stop assuming I might fail, and to stop second guessing myself. It was also a decision to get started *immediately*."

Cass added that the deliberately tight timeline gave her no time to overanalyze the situation, find reasons not to do it, or fall victim to her own "psychological barriers."

So, what was the ad for? A simple housecleaning service.

Cass explained, "I had never cleaned anyone's place but my own, but for once I didn't let anything stop me, and I've been booking consistently for the past 3 months."

She was sick of entrepreneurial advice columns recommending starting a business around your passion. Instead she advised, "For the sake of getting started, I say just pick something you can do."

Can you walk a dog?

Have you ever painted a room?

Think you can handle running errands for old ladies?

"It doesn't really matter what you pick," she added. "The market will tell you if your idea sucks or not."

If you get inquiries right away, you're onto something (possibly) good. If not, then try something else. She urged people to not get caught up in this process, and emphasized that putting yourself out there and getting started are what matter.

One thing that stood out to me was Cass's insistence on *not* thinking of this new venture as a business.

She explained, "Unlike every other time I'd started a business, I didn't feel any pressure to create promotional materials, set up a website, write a business plan, or announce it to the world. In fact, I didn't care whether it succeeded or not."

This is what her first ad said:

*****Competitive Prices / Prix Compétitifs******

Cleaning services for apartments, condos and businesses. Extremely reliable and efficient. I'm looking for people who need regular cleaning. Thanks!

Services de nettoyage pour les appartements, condos etentreprises. Fiable et efficace. Je suis à la recherche de personnes qui ont besoin d'un nettoyage régulièrement. Merci!

****

It's very short and simple. Cass mentioned testing different variations but made one important observation: until you post the first ad, you have nothing to test against.

One thing Cass did to make her ad stand out was to include, in her words, "an attractive picture of a woman." Ads with images tend to get clicked on more, and "most people have bad pictures of themselves or clip art."

She did not recommend putting your own picture up on the site, but instead suggested using a stock photo or royalty-free image of someone who looks like you.

As far as pricing goes, Cass told me she doesn't really have set rates, but her average is about $35 per hour.

"I try not to turn down jobs," she explained. "I speak with my clients to tell them what I can do at the price they're willing to pay, and I take it from there," adding, "I reject clients who try to lowball me or who I find creepy. Remember, this is Craigslist, after all."

Cass sets herself apart with her professionalism. She said potential customers will actually thank her for responding to their messages quickly and politely. Apparently, that's how low the bar is for customer service these days!

But the speed of reply has actually turned out to be an important factor in closing the sale. Cass explained, "I found that the more time I let pass before responding, the less likely a prospect is to hire me."

One great thing about Craigslist is the almost instant gratification, positive or negative. Cass had her first inquiries within an hour of posting her job. If you don't hear anything for a day or two, it's either a sign your service isn't in demand, or it's time to try a new ad.

In either case, Cass cautioned, "Whatever you do, don't give up. Craigslist is full of people looking for services. If I can do it after all my mental blocks and past business failures, I'm sure you can too."

Amazon

Amazon.com is the fourth most popular website in the country and perhaps the largest store in the world. We've already covered how you can put your books up for sale there, but you can add Buy Buttons for physical products as well.

According to a 2015 study, nearly half of all US consumers *start* their product searches on Amazon. The company sold more than $100 billion worth of merchandise last year and boasts over 300 million customers.

And the exciting thing is Amazon actively "crowdsources" its inventory from resellers like you and me. Over 47% of the items Amazon sells are actually sold by third-party sellers who are taking advantage of Amazon's customer base and Buy Buttons.

Amazon lets sellers create their own product listings or add their own items for sale on product pages that already exist. You can do this for new or used inventory, and you can ship the item to the customer yourself when an order comes through or use Amazon's distribution network and have the company ship it for you.

Because I hate going to the post office, I use the Fulfillment by Amazon (FBA) program to deliver orders on my behalf.

There are a couple main ways to tap into the power of Amazon's marketplace as a reseller. The first is similar to the "buy low, sell high" businesses described above, where you aim to acquire inventory—usually new items—cheaply, send them into Amazon's warehouses, and resell them at a profit. This is known as retail or clearance arbitrage. For example, I've dabbled in this business and found profitable clearance products on the shelves at Walmart, Home Depot, Babies 'R Us, and more.

The second model involves creating your own product, usually inspired by a hot-selling item, and having it manufactured. You interface with the factory directly, create your own branding and packaging, and sell the product through Amazon where there's already a proven demand. This is known as private labeling.

In either case, the process is similar. You upload your inventory to your Amazon seller account, set your prices, and package and ship it in bulk to Amazon's distribution center(s). It's essentially stored for you on consignment until it sells, when Amazon ships it out to the customer on your behalf. This has allowed Amazon to significantly increase the breadth of products it sells, while creating a unique Buy Button opportunity for the rest of us as well.

For its effort, Amazon takes a fee on each sale, usually around 30% of the purchase price.

To explore what the Amazon FBA business looks like in practice, I chatted with two professional sellers to get their insight and advice.

Retail Arbitrage

The first seller I connected with was Assad Siddiqi, a finance director for a Boston-area hospital. When we spoke, he was running his Amazon business as a side hustle to his day job, and had managed to resell more than $300,000 worth of retail arbitrage merchandise in under a year.

Like I mentioned, reselling businesses do carry a startup cost to acquire the initial inventory. The beauty of this model, though, is you can begin with whatever amount you're comfortable. In Assad's case, he began with $1500 and said it took 2 months to break even. After that, he just continued to reinvest the profits.

Getting Started

Assad told me the first product he bought was a Barbie closet. He saw these toys on sale for 75% off at his local Target and bought 5 of them. He sold them all on Amazon for 3 times the cost and was hooked.

If you're brand new to this, there are a couple things you need in order to get started. The first is a free Amazon seller account. Amazon also offers a $40/month "professional level" account, which affords you lower fees and faster payouts, but let's keep things lean at the moment.

You can set up your account at sellercentral.amazon.com. Next, you'll want to download the free Amazon Seller app to your phone, and login with your seller account credentials. The app is available for both iOS and Android devices, and the "killer feature" is the barcode reader.

How it Works

How it works is whenever you're out shopping and come across a clearance item, you can scan the barcode with the app to see what that same item is selling for on Amazon. The app will give you the current sales price, your estimated profit after fees, and how many other sellers are selling the product.

How do you know if something's a good buy? The criteria I use is to try and double my money. If I can buy something in the store for $10, I want the estimated profit to be at least $20. The seller app will also often show you the item's sales rank within its category on Amazon, which is a helpful estimator of how quickly the product will sell. My general rule is to look for items with a sales rank of less than 100,000.

For example, the bestselling product in the category has a sales rank of 1, and you know it will sell very quickly. Sometimes I'll buy products with less than the "double my money" rule if I can buy several at once and they have a very low sales rank.

It's important to note that, despite your best efforts, not every product you buy will be profitable and you're putting your dollars at risk by buying the inventory upfront. I've had several purchases where the sales price had dropped on Amazon by the time my inventory got to the warehouse. Other times the items just didn't sell as fast as I thought.

For the first 3-4 months, Assad spent around 20-25 hours a week learning everything he could about the whole process. He pointed out that there is a steep learning curve at first, but finding products that will sell well becomes a lot easier with practice, becoming "almost intuitive" after a few months.

Working Smarter

The frustrating part of this business, at least for me, is the needle-in-a-haystack feeling of it. I hate spending 45 minutes scanning items in a store only to leave empty-handed. You can scan a lot of products before you find a winner, and when there's only one left on the shelf, it's not that big of a win, either.

I asked Assad what he did to combat that and make sure he uses his limited time as efficiently as possible. He told me he implemented 3 processes to help speed up his business:

1. Using paid services to find products easier and quicker
2. Sourcing products online instead of in stores
3. Delegating parts of his work load

Assad explained there are a handful of paid services where you can buy curated lists of items that someone else has researched for you as having potential for profit. For example, I'm a member of the Sourcing Simplifiers Facebook group, and I often see lists offered for sale.

(Assad also helps run SourcingSimplifiers.com, a blog and resource for people getting started in the Amazon FBA business.)

You can then do your own due diligence, look for these products at stores near you, or buy them online. In fact, Assad said that online sourcing turned into a major win for him. As someone who used to run a comparison shopping site, I was surprised to hear this. If buyers could get a product significantly cheaper a few mouse clicks away, why were they still buying on Amazon for an inflated price?

Assad pointed to the fact that Amazon has built up huge trust with buyers. Also, many of them are Prime customers and simply start their product search on Amazon; they aren't looking around at other sites.

For this "online arbitrage," Assad recommended a Chrome browser extension called OAXray (oaxray.com). This tool scans pages of products and compares them to their sale price on Amazon for you. OAXray requires a $99/month subscription fee but comes with a 3-day free trial to test the software.

The advantage of online sourcing is it saves a ton of time compared with driving around to different stores, and often you can get multiple units of a product at once instead of just the last one on the shelf at Walmart.

The other area where Assad has freed up his time is in delegating some of the workload. After a successful sourcing trip, the next step is to typically input all the items into your Amazon seller account, package them up, and ship them off to Amazon. I can tell you first-hand this is a time-consuming process that fills your living room up with boxes and packing supplies.

Instead, Assad started to use a "prep and pack" company to handle all of his inspecting, labeling, boxing, and posting to Amazon. To him, the sourcing is the fun part, and that's where the money is made, not in the logistics and packaging. "If I'm not sourcing inventory, I'm not making money," he explained.

There are prep-and-pack companies all over the country, and once you have an established relationship with one, you can actually send your online orders directly to the facility without ever touching the product.

To get a better understanding of the business and be surrounded by likeminded people, Assad recommended getting involved in some of the Amazon FBA Facebook groups. In addition to the Sourcing Simplifiers group mentioned above, he recommended the Scanpower Facebook group and the FBA Masters Facebook group.

In addition to getting access to the paid sourcing lists, you'll also find a helpful community of other resellers sharing their tips and answering questions.

The natural progression for a lot of FBA side hustlers is to move from reselling products they find to importing products and creating their own private label brands. Assad hasn't done this yet, but indicated he may do so in the future.

Private Labeling

To learn more about importing and private labeling, I sat down with Greg Mercer, a 7-figure Amazon seller. Greg knows the reselling business inside and out, and even created a software tool called Jungle Scout to help new sellers discover profitable products.

Greg told me it's "super easy" to get started with FBA. "The marketplace is already thriving," he explained, "And new sellers are finding success every day."

I told him about my retail arbitrage efforts and the results that Assad had seen, and Greg said that was a great way to learn how Amazon works and get a taste for the volume of sales that flow through its marketplace every day. The other advantages he mentioned were lower upfront investments, not having to create your own product listings from scratch, and not really having to worry about marketing the product.

Yet Greg advocated private labeling as a way to tap into economies of scale and the full potential of

Amazon's audience of buyers. If you can sell 1,000 units of a product and make $10 apiece, he asked, doesn't that sound better than tediously scanning items at Target, hoping to find one that will make a few bucks?

I would describe private labeling as higher risk, higher reward than retail arbitrage. How it works is you identify a product or product concept you think will sell, contact a manufacturer (often in China to keep costs low), make a bulk order, and finally use Amazon's fulfillment system to ship orders to the end customer.

Product Research

It's a much more involved process from start to finish, but it always begins with product research.

Greg admitted that coming up with a product idea is probably the hardest part. To help narrow down the process, I asked him what criteria he uses when looking for a product to manufacture. He gave me the following guidelines:

- **Small and lightweight.** This keeps shipping costs and Amazon handling fees down. The ideal product should be able to fit into a shoebox and not weigh more than a few pounds.
- **Not breakable.** Shipping from China to the US and then to an Amazon distribution center will have its share of bumps.

- **Designed simply.** Select a product with few moving parts, as this reduces the chances of faulty items and returns.
- **Sell for $20-50.** This ensures there is enough profit to make it worthwhile. Below that, and it will be hard to recoup shipping costs, and above that, buyers may be a little more brand sensitive.
- **Not patented and un-licensed**. Items with major brand or organization names on them can cause legal issues. For instance, that sweet Chewbacca hoodie or that cute Captain America shield backpack are probably no good.
- **Low liability.** Choose products that do not pose any health risks to the user. That means medical devices or skydiving accessories are probably out as well.

Greg recently launched a new product and featured it on his blog (JungleScout.com/blog) as an example. The product? Bamboo marshmallow sticks branded as "Jungle Stix." They're an excellent example of a product that fits all of his criteria above, except at 36 inches long they don't fit in a shoe box.

Still, the bamboo sticks are lightweight, are virtually unbreakable in transit, feature an incredibly simple design, sell for $27.99, and pose no patent or licensing issues, even though Greg didn't invent them.

Greg told me he sold 245 bundles of these sticks, which come in a 110 pack, in the first month of sales, profiting around $8 per box, or around $2,000 net profit for the month. Not bad for some long sticks to hold marshmallows on the end!

Greg also pointed out that in this case the sticks were already being manufactured in the factory he contacted. That meant he didn't incur any research and development costs with this product, but only had to create the "Jungle Stix" branding and packaging.

"The key is finding an opportunity within the market, then finding a manufacturer," he explained.

"So how do I find that opportunity in the market?" I asked.

Finding Product Ideas

Greg said this is where most people get stuck, and he shared some tips on how he finds products and what works best for beginners. "The important thing to remember when looking for product ideas is you aren't trying to reinvent the wheel," he explained. "What I try and do is find products that are *already* selling well on Amazon, are proven to be in demand, and fit with the criteria above."

Greg recommended starting with a Google search for "amazon best sellers," which will bring up a dedicated best-seller page that's hard to find otherwise, and then drilling down by the various categories. He mentioned some categories are more "beginner friendly" than others, including:

- Sports and Outdoors
- Home and Kitchen
- Patio, Lawn, and Garden
- Pet Supplies

When you find a category you are interested in, niche down into a subcategory to increase your chance of finding the less competitive products.

Once he finds a product that looks compelling based on the size/weight/price criteria above, he looks at two other factors:

- Estimated sales volume
- Number of reviews

To get an estimate of the sales volume, Greg and his team built a tool at JungleScout.com/estimator that tells you roughly how many units are being sold per month if you type in the sales rank. He suggested searching for similar products and using the estimator tool to add up the estimated sales volume of the top 10 best sellers.

If the sum estimated sales of those 10 products is around 3,000 units per month, that's what Greg calls his sweet spot. He said he's found if he launches his own private label product to compete with those, he can expect to sell around 300 units a month.

The other consideration is the number of reviews each of these products has. He explained, "If at least one of the top 5 products has less than 100 reviews and if a few of the top 10 have less than 100 reviews, this is a very good indication that the product is either fairly new, or the competition is low enough to enter the market."

Manufacturing

Once you have decided on a product, you need to find a manufacturer. Alibaba.com is by far the largest online marketplace for finding suppliers. Most are based in China, and this is where Greg orders all his products as it's the most cost-effective place for manufacturing.

I asked Greg how to find a good, reliable supplier in the overwhelming directory of Alibaba. He said he starts with a keyword search (bamboo sticks, for example), to find what manufacturers are already producing items like the one he's looking for.

He advised to set up a new email account to avoid spam from aggressive factory reps, and then he sends a basic inquiry to 5-10 different suppliers. In that initial email, he asks what their minimum order quantities are and if they're willing to send him a sample of the product.

What he's *really* looking for, he explained, aside from answers to those questions, is to see how well they communicate in English and what kind of gut feeling they give off.

When you have a factory you're comfortable with (or a couple), request some samples of the product so you can inspect them for quality and consistency. If you're happy with the samples, it's time to place your first bulk order and negotiate the best price possible.

Greg said he likes to order a minimum of 1,000 units. "I always run out of product when I purchase only 250 or 500 units," he explained. "But," he added, "if 1,000 units seems like a scary investment at first, just go with what you're comfortable with." Depending on the price of your product, that could mean an initial investment of $500 to $5,000 or more.

The other thing to keep in mind is this can be a slow process. There is typically a lead time of at least 30 days from placing an order to receiving the product.

On to Amazon

The manufacturing and shipping time is a good opportunity to work on your packaging and labeling. You may be able to create the labels yourself or find a freelancer to help design your product packaging. How "high-end" do you want your product to look? Do you want to go all in with the "Apple experience" of luxurious packaging or keep it simple?

Greg suggested creating a placeholder product listing in your Amazon seller account at this time, which will generate the required FNSKU you can use on your labels.

Once you have the products in hand, make sure to inspect them for quality. Then it's time to pack them up and ship them off to Amazon to handle as part of its FBA process.

With private labeling, you have control over your product page, including the title and description text, the photos, and the price. There's a lot of strategy that goes into marketing your product and collecting reviews once it's on Amazon, but Greg assured me the only way to learn is by doing it. He encouraged readers to take it one step at a time and solve the unique challenges as they come up.

I believe we're still in the early days of ecommerce. Even just a few years ago it would have been almost unheard of for individuals to interact directly with Chinese factories, have their own products made from scratch, and put them up for sale to an audience of 300 million buyers on Amazon.

Greg acknowledged that the Amazon FBA business is becoming more crowded and competitive, but he is bullish about its future. In addition to the main US market, he said, "There is also a lot of potential for selling products in emerging markets like the UK, Germany, Canada, and Mexico on the horizon."

The biggest advantage of Amazon I see is as an accelerator. Yes, you're paying the company a fee on every unit that sells, but you're borrowing the trust it's been building with customers for 20 years. Of course it would be awesome to have your own ecommerce storefront—and for many Amazon sellers, that's the next level—but you don't need one to get started.

Bonus: Want to learn more about starting an ecommerce business? Download the free Ecommerce bonus at BuyButtonsBook.com/bonus.

Inside you'll find examples of how to find hot products to sell, how to set up your own online store, and how to drive profitable traffic.

Specialty Marketplaces for Physical Goods

While it may make sense to cast as wide a net as possible when reselling items, there are some specialty marketplaces to be aware of if you have products in certain categories.

For instance, I've had better luck buying and selling phones on Swappa.com than on eBay. Because it specializes only in phones, there's less "junk" to filter out, and it has unique features in place that protect both parties. As a seller, the flat $10 sales fee is more attractive than paying eBay $40 on the sale of a $400 phone as well.

Other Platforms to Consider

ThredUp – ThredUp.com will send you a free "Clean Out Kit" to send in your unused clothes for consignment sale. You can even use the online payout estimator tool to see what your items are worth.

Poshmark – Sell your designer clothes through the Poshmark.com app, which makes it easy to photograph and list an item in just 60 seconds.

Swap.com – Sell your women's and children's clothes through Swap's online consignment store and earn an average of $150 for each box of clothes you send in.

Swap Style – Save money by borrowing or buying used designer clothes on SwapStyle.com. Or sell from your own closet.

BagBorroworSteal – Sell your designer handbags and accessories on consignment, or take a lower offer price and get paid right away.

Depop – The Depop.com mobile app allows you to sell items from your closet and upload pictures and descriptions. I definitely get an Instagram vibe on the site as there's an emphasis on great-looking photography. Depop says it's facilitated "tens of millions" of transactions since 2012.

SidelineSwap – SidelineSwap.com is an online marketplace for athletes to buy, sell, and trade gear.

Chairish – Marketplace for design-lovers to buy and sell vintage and used furniture, décor, and art.

TradingCradles.com – Parents can buy and sell baby gear as their little ones get bigger and bigger.

Conclusion and Next Steps

In many ways, this book is Marketing 101: get in front of your customers where they already are. Who are they already doing business with? How can you put your Buy Button where they'll find it?

When I was in college, I shadowed a real estate agent for a day in Seattle. As a marketing major, I asked what he did to help market and sell these million-dollar homes he specialized in.

What he said surprised me. "I hold open houses and take out newspaper ads because that's what clients expect and it's something tangible they can see," he explained, "but the truth is probably 90% of sales come through listing the property on the MLS (multiple listing service)."

That was a compelling testament to the power of marketplaces. Despite all his other marketing efforts, the single most effective sales tactic was putting his Buy Button where buyers (and their agents) were looking.

In this book I focused on online marketplaces, but the strategy works offline as well. Where else can you put your Buy Buttons? The bulletin board at your gym? The hallways of your school? In my businesses, I'm always thinking of ways I can shrink the universe down to where I can get in front of the exact people I want to see me.

These marketplaces reduce the friction between buyers and sellers, between entrepreneurs and customers. They make it easy for people to do business with each other.

We covered a huge variety of sharing economy platforms, where you can turn the underutilized assets in your life into cash.

Next, we looked at dozens of specialty marketplaces where you can sell your skills either as a freelancer or packaged up as physical or digital products.

And finally, we explored the largest reselling marketplaces where you can tap into audiences of millions of buyers using the age-old "buy low, sell high" business model.

Your Homework

Your mission now, should you choose to accept it, is **to pick one platform** to add your Buy Button to, take action, and let me know your results. I'd love to add your story to the next edition of this book!

Don't get overwhelmed with all the choices. Remember, action is the first step toward seeing results and building positive momentum. If your first marketplace selection doesn't work for you, don't get discouraged. There are literally hundreds of others to try and a whole world of buyers out there ready to do business with you.

Ryan Finlay, the Craigslist reseller you met a moment ago, left me with some of the best advice I've ever heard: *"The best opportunities are only visible once you're in motion."*

In my 15+ years as an entrepreneur, I know this to be true. The projects I'm working on today are the direct result of (often) completely unrelated actions taken in the past. My shoe business started when I took a part-time marketing internship. Another one of my websites started when I was doing research for a different (failed) project. Heck, this book idea started as a blog post!

Action breeds action.

Once you're in motion, all of a sudden new ideas and opportunities become visible.

It's a strange phenomenon, but perhaps the best explanation for it I've heard is my friend Julie's analogy. She explained that starting a business is like a game of chess, in that your first move doesn't really matter. All you're trying to do is move your pawn out into the world and see what kind of reaction it gets.

So back to your homework assignment: **pick one platform today** and get started.

Keep the Conversation Going

If you'd like to join a supportive and active community of other entrepreneurs and side hustlers, please join the free Side Hustle Nation Facebook group:

SideHustleNation.com/fb

You'll be able to ask questions, help others on their journey, and share your victories along the way.

Liked the Book?

If you liked *Buy Buttons*, it would mean the world to me if you took a moment to leave an honest review on Amazon. Thank you!

Reader Bonus

Don't forget, as a small token of gratitude for you reading this book, I've compiled a few bonuses for you. These are meant to complement the content of the book, help you save money, and take a deeper dive into the business models you're most interested in.

- $1150 in free "sharing economy" discounts and credits
- The Freelancing and Consulting Bonus: How to get your first clients and position yourself for big paydays.
- The Online Teaching Bonus: How to get paid to share your expertise with others.
- The Ecommerce Bonus: How to start a profitable business selling products online.

To download your free bonuses, you head over to **BuyButtonsBook.com/bonus.**

Thanks and Acknowledgements

A project like this really does take a village. I'd like to thank the dozens of people who supported the creation of this book and helped me along the way.

Editing: Bryn Miyahara and Elizabeth Stockton.

Cover Design: Bulan Arafika from DesignCrowd.com.

Case Studies: Matt Bochnak, Dave Bredeson, Lise Cartwright, Dillon Casey, Tyler Castleman, Elizabeth Colegrove, Mario DiBartolomeo, Marie Dolphin, Phil Ebiner, Ryan Finlay, Darrel Fitzpatrick, Ben Foley, Gina Galligan, Jesse Gernigin, Kevin Ha, Anna Hamill, Chad Hansen, Dan Houseman, Kevin Howard, Janelle Jones, Alexandra Kenin, Dan Khadem, Nicky Laatz, Michael Lam, Kara Lamerato, Mike Marani, Aja McClanahan, Greg Mercer, Robert Murray, Mike Naab, Catherine Nissen, Carrie Olsen, Shreyans Parekh, Kat Parrella, Cassandre Poblah, Jasper Ribbers, Molly Rosen, Janet Saunderson, Assad Siddiqi, Leez Snow, Sean Sumner, Rob Stephenson, Scott Tarcy, Anand Thangavel, Kevin Thomas, Jose Vieitez, Gabby Wallace, and Jeff Yenisch.

Connectors: Diana Adair, Rafael Beyer, Chandler Bolt, Kevin Bradford, Alexea Candreva, Alexandra Constantine, Jeffrey Dobin, John Lee Dumas, Gen

Furukawa, Jake Jolis, Sam Mellor, Nikolaj Nielsen, Touran Samii, Tara Wagner, and Danny Weiss.

Launch Team: Nadia Aftab, Hussain Ahmed, Diane Aksten, Mike Amos, Sarah Anderson, Brian Ardón, Andrew Baker, Brendan Alan Barrett, Ken Biller, Mark Bologna, Lisa Bonanno, Hannah Braime, Kris Broholm, James Burrus, Jenell Butler, Bob Choat, Jonathan Churchill, Fran Civile, Douglas Glenn Clark, Jason Connolly, Brandon Cullum, Doug Cunnington, Debashish Das, Patrik Edblad, Lyuba Ellingson, Mark Enders, Theodore Evans, Samantha Fairclough, Thayde Garavito, Megan Garrison, Melissa Gartner, Michel Gerard, Tony Griego, Linda Griffin, Lee Hills, Don Holliday, Kyle Humiston, Dianne Humphries, James Hundley, Bridget Hunt, Dorin Ionescu, Jaime Jay, Bob Johnson, Marcia Kelley, Naveed Kharrat, Wade Kutella, Michele Lashley, Angela Leigh, Valérie Leroyer, Dror Lewy, Kevin Love, Jayme Martin, Toby Martinez, Liz Massey, Tim McAuley, Tamara McCray, Dan McDaniel, Kathleen McDivitt, Jim Medina, Judy Menting, Steve Meza, Larisa Lambert Mills, Jimmy Moncrief, Dave Mooring, Wachira Mwendia, Chris Naish, Linda Nevin, Marie Ong, Jocelyn Orozco, Andrew Perkins, Joanna Pieters, Cameron Potter, Christel Price, Raul Ramirez, John Rasmussen, Nimisha Reddy, Nicole Reid, Laurel Rolls, Emily Roth, Matthew Scarlett, Cathy Schwab, Brett Simpson, Lucas Smatana, Emily Chase Smith, Jaimi Sorrell, Steve Spring, John Stavropoulos, Mohana Suntharan, Renita Terry, Michael Thornhill, Michele Tocci, Carmen Toft, Mark Tune, David Tweats, Brian

Walker, Tim Warren, Gwendolyn Stanton Whitfield, Brittney Young, Eric Zartan, and Lukasz Zymer.

Marketing Support: Tyler Basu, Zephan Blaxberg, Chandler Bolt, Dave Chesson, Dorie Clark, Bryan Cohen, Rob Cubbon, Derek Doepker, Steph Halligan, Joseph Hogue, Stephen Key, Jesse Krieger, Hahna Kane Latonick, Sally Miller, Tom Morkes, Derek Murphy, Cathy Presland, Austin Netzley, Jyotsna Ramachandran, Natalie Sisson, Mish Slade, Steve Scott, Michal Stawicki, Brandon Turner, and Ellory Wells.

References

Alexa. "Site Info: eBay." Web.

BLS.gov. "Entrepreneurship and the U.S. Economy." Web.

CBC News. "400 UberX vehicles seized so far this year in Montreal." *CBC News*, 6 Nov. 2015. Web.

Desilver, Drew. "For most workers, real wages have barely budged for decades." Pew Research Center, 9 Oct. 2014. Web.

El Issa, Erin. "2015 American Household Credit Card Debt Study." *Nerdwallet*, Web.

Gale, Sadie Levy. "How to rent your house out - without the hassle of guests staying overnight." *The Telegraph*, 21 Jan. 2016. Web.

Griswold, Alison. "The verdict on the "sharing" economy, from the 20% of Americans who've worked in it." *Quartz*, 7 Jan. 2016. Web.

Greenberg, Jon. "47% say they lack ready cash to pay a surprise $400 bill." *Politifact*, 9 Jun. 2015. Web.

Kelley, Donna, Slavica Singer, and Mike Herrington. Global Entrepreneurship Monitor 2015/16 Global Report. Web.

Li, David K. "Majority of city's Airbnb rentals last year were illegal: report." *New York Post*, 28 Jun. 2016. Web.

Marvin, Ginny. "Amazon Is the Starting Point For 44 Percent Of Consumers Searching For Products. Is Google Losing, Then?." *Marketing Land*, 8 Oct. 2015. Web.

McCue, TJ. "Online Learning Industry Poised for $107 Billion In 2015." *Forbes*, 27 Aug. 2014. Web.

Meyer, Jared. "Millennials Want To Be Entrepreneurs, So Why Aren't They Starting Businesses? Part 1." *Forbes*, 20 Jul. 2015. Web.

My Budget 360. "Comparing the cost of living between 1975 and 2015." Web.

NASA.gov. "InnoCentive Investigation of the Challenge Driven Innovation Platform at NASA." 25 Oct. 2010. Web.

Pickell, Jim. "Top Myths of the Sharing Economy." *Huffington Post*, 13 Jan. 2016. Web.

Piper, Ally. "Make Money from Your Photos: A Beginner's Guide to Selling Stock Photography." *The Penny Hoarder*, 4 Aug. 2014. Web.

Rossa, Jennifer and Anne Riley. "These Charts Show
　　　How the Sharing Economy Is Different."
　　　Bloomberg, 15 Jul. 2015. Web.

Schrader, Brendon. "Here's Why The Freelancer
　　　Economy Is On The Rise." *Fast Company*, 10
　　　Aug. 2015. Web.

Smith, Craig. "By the Numbers: 40 Amazing Etsy
　　　Statistics." *DMR*, 14 Jul. 2016. Web.

Statista. "eBay's gross merchandise volume from 2nd
　　　quarter 2014 to 2nd quarter 2016 (in billion
　　　U.S. dollars)." Web.

Statista. "Statistics and facts about Amazon." Web.

Steinmetz, Katy. "Exclusive: See How Big the Gig
　　　Economy Really Is." *Time*, 6 Jan. 2016. Web.

U.S. Chamber of Commerce Foundation. "The
　　　Millennial Generation Research Review." Web.

About the Author

Nick Loper is an online entrepreneur and lifelong student in the game of business. He lives in Northern California with his wife Bryn, son Max, and a lovable giant Shih-Tzu called Mochi. On a typical day you can find him writing, working on his latest business idea, rooting for the Huskies, or skiing the Sierra pow.

Nick has witnessed the power of the Buy Buttons strategy many times over, until it finally hit him that he should write a book about it.

As you can probably tell from the book, he gets really excited about this stuff and wants to help others find success online.

Want to know more?

Drop by and check out his blog and podcast at SideHustleNation.com, a growing resource and community for aspiring and part-time entrepreneurs.

Connect with fellow side hustlers to share wins, get feedback, and support each in the free Facebook group:

SideHustleNation.com/fb

Do you have a *Buy Buttons* success story to share? Get in touch (nick@sidehustlenation.com), and you might just be featured in the next edition of this book!

Also by Nick

Nick is also the author of:

The Side Hustle Path: 10 Proven Ways to Make Money Outside of Your Day Job

The Side Hustle Path Volume 2: 10 Proven Ways to Make Money Outside of Your Day Job

The Side Hustle Path Volume 3: 10 Proven Ways to Make Money Outside of Your Day Job

The Side Hustle Path Volume 4: 10 Proven Ways to Make Money Outside of Your Day Job

The Small Business Website Checklist: A 51-Point Guide to Build Your Online Presence The Smart Way

Treadmill Desk Revolution: The Easy Way to Lose Up to 50 Pounds in a Year – Without Dieting

Virtual Assistant Assistant: The Ultimate Guide to Finding, Hiring, and Working with Virtual Assistants

Work Smarter: 500+ Online Resources Today's Top Entrepreneurs Use to Increase Productivity and Achieve Their Goals

Printed in Great Britain
by Amazon